Sex and Advantage

Sex and Advantage
A Comparative, Macro-Structural Theory of Sex Stratification

Janet Saltzman Chafetz

Rowman & Allanheld
PUBLISHERS

ROWMAN & ALLANHELD

Published in the United States of America in 1984
by Rowman & Allanheld, Publishers
(A division of Littlefield, Adams & Company)
81 Adams Drive, Totowa, New Jersey 07512

Chafetz, Janet Saltzman.
    Sex and advantage.

    Bibliography: p.
    Includes index.
    1. Sex and discrimination against women.   2. Social
structure.   3. Discrimination in employment.   4. Family.
5. Multivariate analysis.   I. Title.
HQ21.C449   1983   305.4'2   83-19077
ISBN 0-86598-159-0
ISBN 0-86598-161-2 (pbk.)

84 85 86 / 10 9 8 7 6 5 4 3 2 1

Printed in the United States of America

CONTENTS

FIGURES

PREFACE

This book represents a synthesis of my twin interests in sex inequality and formal theory. For a decade I have been increasingly perturbed by two failures: the failure of most sociological theorists to devote serious attention to understanding the important and universal phenomenon of sex stratification, and the failure of most sociologists interested in gender and sex inequality to develop cross-cultural, macro-level, testable theories of sex stratification. The theorists fail to recognize the importance of the substantive issue, while the gender specialists overlook the importance of formal theory. Indeed, it appears that the vast majority of American sociologists interested in issues concerning gender are fundamentally social psychologists. Only in recent years have some scholars turned their attention to the macro-level of analysis, not in order to understand individual behavior better, but to understand structural phenomena in their own right.

The degree to which males and females are equal in their access to societal scarce values, i.e., the extent of sex stratification, is a structural variable. From an individual's perspective, the structural characteristics of his/her society have important ramifications for all aspects of life. Moreover, structural features of societies are, or at least ought to be, intrinsically interesting to sociologists. Indeed, the explanation of a structural feature is to be found in examining other structural, not individual-level, phenomena. Environmental, technological, and demographic characteristics of societies shape responses in terms of how productive activities and families are structured. In turn, the ways in which societies organize families and productive labor impact their sex stratification systems and, through feedback, are influenced by the systems of sex inequality. This is the central thesis of this work. Individuals *are* impacted by structure, but the understanding of structure is not enhanced by the study of individuals. It is incumbent upon those who wish to eliminate the problems created by structured sex inequality to understand better the roots of that structure. It should be noted that individual opportunity levels are clearly a function of a variety of variables other than sex (e.g., class, race). In this book, these other structural sources of social inequality are implicitly "held constant" and attention is centered solely on sex.

Almost all the ideas presented here have been expressed elsewhere by others. To my knowledge, however, they have never been systematically integrated into a unified theory to explain variance in the degree of sex inequality cross-culturally and historically. The amount of speculative, largely mono-causal "theory" is substantial, while potentially testable, multi-causal theory in the area is scarce. To present the latter I have relied upon the data, interpretations, and insights of scores of social scientists, especially sociologists and anthropologists. Those who influenced me most are indicated by the number of times they are referenced in the pages that follow. I also owe a long-standing intellectual debt to Joseph Lopreato and Jack Gibbs for impressing upon me the importance and utility of formal theory.

My deepest appreciation is owed to Elizabeth Almquist, A. Gary Dworkin, Desley Deacon, David Gottlieb, and Judy Corder for critiquing an earlier draft of this manuscript. Their help was enormous, and any remaining errors or shortcomings are mine. Thanks are also due to several people for their encouragement, moral support, and faith in this project: Henry Chafetz, Gladys Topkis, Helen Ebaugh, Joseph Kotarba, and Alan Stone. Finally, I wish to thank the University of Houston Publication Committee for a typing grant, Ciro Ribeiro for typing the manuscript, and the University of Houston, College of Social Sciences Public Policy Center, for defraying other manuscript preparation costs.

1

DEFINING THE ISSUES

It may be a truism to say that in most societies all women are not equal. Yet it is equally true that in few, if any, societies are women as a category equal to men considered categorically. And it is certainly the case that the *degree* to which women are disadvantaged varies extensively across time and space, but that nowhere, apparently, are women superior to men in overall status. This book is an effort to develop a general theoretical understanding of why societies differ in the degree of inequality between the sexes, and an insight into why women have apparently never been more advantaged in their access to scarce and valued societal resources.

Since 1973, when Acker decried the lack of attention paid to sex as a stratification variable, sex has been added to wealth, occupational prestige, power, race and ethnicity as a general dimension of stratification. Some have defined sex in terms of castes (Andreas 1971; Chafetz 1978: 114–15), others as minority-majority groups (Dworkin 1976; Hacker 1951; Myrdal 1944), a few even in terms of classes (Laws 1975). Regardless of which rubric is employed, most social scientists today agree that it is a pertinent variable in understanding social inequality. While the methodology necessary to study some aspects of stratification and social mobility in terms of sex may be crude or altogether lacking, recognition is now widespread that an individual's access to the scarce and valued resources of her/his society is affected as much, if not more, by sex as by the more traditional stratification variables considered by sociologists.

On the individual level, one's access to the scarce and valued resources of society (i.e., one's position in the stratification hierarchy) is the result of her/his profile on a variety of possible dimensions: wealth, education, race/ethnicity, religion, age, family status, occupational status, etc. Societies differ extensively on the number and kinds of these dimensions, but in almost all human societies sex constitutes one such dimension,

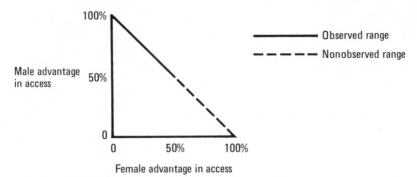

Figure 1.1   **Possible Degrees of Advantage in Access to Societal Scarce and Valued Resources, by Sex**

and typically one of the more important ones. Yet extensive variability does exist in the *degree* to which sex influences access, i.e., the extent to which males and females, on the basis of sex alone, are unequal. In this book, the other dimensions that provide individual opportunity levels will be implicitly held constant while the dimension of sex is examined.

It is logically possible for societies to vary from extreme inequality advantaging females, through sexual equality, to extreme inequality advantaging males. Nevertheless, when societies are examined empirically, it becomes evident that the range of sexual inequality is truncated. In Figure 1.1, relative advantage in access to societal scarce and valued resources is conceptualized as ranging from 0 to 100 percent for each sex, the percentage indicating the extent to which one sex is advantaged over the other. If males are advantaged at the rate of 100 percent, females are totally disadvantaged, i.e., have a score of 0 percent, and vice versa. As the advantage of one sex decreases, the access advantage of the other sex increases in exact proportion, since the total must always be 100 percent. At the two extremes, the only access members of the sex scoring zero have is through their attachment to members of the other sex. In reality, however, the part of the figure represented by a dashed line has never been observed empirically. Thus, the reality in need of explanation is that represented as ranging from nearly total male dominance of access to relative equality between the sexes in such access. In the process of explaining the empirically variable part of this continuum, the reasons for the constant finding—that nowhere are females more advantaged than males—may also become clear.

Many theories of sexual inequality pose the wrong question. Instead of asking what variables account for variation in *degree* of sex inequality, they address the issues of "How did the subordination of women to men come about?" or "What accounts for female subordination to males?" The first question presupposes an era in history in which females were not subordinated to males; the second assumes that females have always been subordinated; and both utilize a simple dichotomy—subordination vs. non-subordination. Answers to such questions range from neo-Marxist discussions of the influence of private property and capitalism on the development of "patriarchy"; to speculations concerning male use of force (i.e., rape) or genetically based male bonding to subordinate women, the sublimation of male "womb envy" into dominance in nonreproductive spheres of life, or greater male libidinal energy; to sociobiological analyses of "selfish genes" and male maximization of their genetic inheritance through control of females. The number of such theoretical speculations is vast. To the extent that some of these insights are useful in developing a general theory of sex stratification, they will be used where relevant. I shall not, however, review each fully, only to point out their shortcomings.

These speculative theories tend to share several common problems. First, they are generally incapable of generating testable hypotheses, in large measure because most have no dependent variable; they tend to be attempts to explain a constant—female subordination—which is in fact a variable, the degree of female disadvantage. Second, they tend to be mono-causal, emphasizing one biological, economic, or psychological factor to account for a very complex set of institutional phenomena. Third, most are based heavily, if implicitly, on assumptions, speculations or, at the very least, unverifiable assertions concerning either the basic nature of one or both sexes or the nature of human societies in the prehistorical past—or both. Finally, many are based on vaguely defined concepts often ill suited to operationalization, such as "patriarchy," "female subordination," and "sexism." The use of such emotion-laden but unclear terms, combined typically with a heavily normative approach to the topic of sex inequality, results in a maximum of rhetoric but a minimum of clear insight.

In recent years several scholars have begun to address the theoretical task of explaining variation in degree of sex stratification across societies, which implicitly includes historical variations as well (e.g., Blumberg 1978, 1979; Martin and Voorhies 1975; Nielsen 1978; O'Kelly 1980; Rosaldo 1974; and Sanday 1974). These various authors show considerable convergence, and those who published most recently often draw heavily upon the work of anthropologists Martin and Voorhies. Most approach the issue by examining different societal *types* in terms of variations in sex inequality. The societal types employed tend to follow Lenski's (1966) approach, and types are distinguished on the basis of the level of technology and the amount of surplus production possible at that level of technology. Typically, societies are categorized as hunting/gathering (or foraging), simple horticultural, advanced horticultural, agrarian, and industrial. Two stages of the industrial may be defined, an earlier and a postindustrial, and in some instances pastoral societies are treated separately. Among modern industrial societies, in addition to level of technology and degree of surplus production, distinctions frequently are made according to political economy: the (more-or-less) capitalistic West and the socialistic or communistic East. Often the relative status of women in dependent or Third World societies is examined separately, as well.

To approach the issue of what accounts for variation in degree of sex stratification through examination and comparison of societal types, however defined, obscures the relative impact of a series of general variables on degree of sex inequality. Types themselves are inherently incapable of directly explaining anything; they are fundamentally descriptive devices. Explanation requires a series of unidimensional variables, although they may tend to be highly related to one another and to societal types. The questions to be posed in this work concern, for instance, the effects of family size, the division of household labor, degree of female involvement in economically productive activities, and a myriad of other variables on the relative status of women and men. The possible answers to such questions are implicit in the existing work cited, but are nowhere stated as a set of clear propositions, not to mention a systematic theory, amenable to testing.

It is the purpose of this book to develop a theory based not on societal types, which are used rather for exemplary purposes, but on general or universal variables; i.e., to develop a general theory of sex stratification by utilizing universally applicable variables. The theory is multivariate and systemic in nature and is an example of what Mayhew (1980) defines as the "structuralist approach." It is also an elaboration of a paper published a few years ago (Chafetz 1980c). Examples justifying theoretical relationships will be cited, as will data that test specific portions of the theory that have been published by others.

Sex Stratification Defined

Common sense tells us that female status is inferior to that of males. Yet when one considers the range of different societal types, one notes that the ways in which such inequality may be manifested vary enormously. In the most general sense, degree of stratification (including the specific case of sex stratification) refers to the extent to which societal members are unequal in their access to the scarce values of their society.

The concept "sex stratification" refers to a comparison of access levels by the two sexes within a given society at a given time. Studies of female status often compare females in one society or at one historical time with females in one or more different societies or at another time, on one or more dimensions such as income, education, legal rights, etc. Such a practice is highly misleading and, in fact, tells us nothing about sex stratification per se. If females in society "A" are better off than females in society "B" on some variable(s), it may well be because all members of society "A" are advantaged relative to all members of society "B." Even so, it is still possible that sex stratification is greater in society "A" than "B."

There are few, if any, universally valid indicators of sex inequality. For example in societies based on money (as are almost all today), income is one good indicator, but not all societies are or have been based on money, and societies vary in degree. In societies with formal decision-making roles, relative access to such roles can serve as one indicator of equality, but not all societies have had formal decision-making roles. To test any theory employing degree of sex stratification as a variable, relatively arbitrary decisions would have to be made in operationalizing the variable "degree of sex inequality." It would probably be impossible to develop a detailed, interval, or ratio scale of inequality that is a valid indicator of the total concept. What is probably possible, however, is a composite measure that will allow a researcher to divide societies into several ordinal levels of inequality, ranging from nearly total equality to nearly total male dominance.

What are the main conceptual (not operational) dimensions of sex inequality? A list of such dimensions follows, i.e., a list of the scarce values to which societal members may have differential (unequal) access on the basis of sex. The reader may wish to add other dimensions; this list does not exhaust the logical possibilities, although it is intended to include the most important ones, and certainly those most frequently considered in the literature:

1. degree of access to the material goods available in the society;
2. degree of access to services provided by others;
3. degree of access to educational and/or training opportunities;
4. degree of access to public decision-making (formal power and authority);
5. degree of access to interpersonal, including familial, decision-making (informal power and authority);
6. degree of access to prestige-conferring roles;
7. degree of access to opportunities for psychic enrichment and gratification;

8. degree of access to discretionary time;

9. degree of freedom from behavioral constraints, including physically constraining clothing and norms concerning "proper" behavior;

10. degree of formal rights granted by the society to its members; and

11. degree of access to life-sustaining requisites, including food and medical care, and freedom from physical coercion (assault and homocide), including infanticide.

This list illustrates that the development of an adequate measure of degree of sex inequality, one that is cross-culturally and historically valid, is a complex undertaking. Since this study is an attempt to develop a theory, in the rest of this book it will be assumed that, at some level, such measurement is possible, and that this variable represents a composite of these various dimensions into one "score" for each society, however that composite is actually developed.

It is also apparent from this list that simple measures of sex inequality that rely only on income, occupational prestige, education, and/or formal political power may be misleading when applied cross-culturally, and that males and females may suffer from different forms of disadvantage or advantage that are missed by too-simple measurements. It should be added, however, that to the extent that females are highly disadvantaged in terms of income, education, occupational prestige, and formal power, the greatest likelihood is that they will be more disadvantaged than males on many, if not most, of the other dimensions, as well. Blumberg (1979) has conceptualized three types of "power": political, coercive and, for the analysis of sex stratification the most important, economic. She argues that the relative economic power of the sexes stands at the root of all other dimensions of sex inequality.

Nonetheless, it is possible that the extent of female disadvantage has been exaggerated by a failure to take into account some of the dimensions, such as informal power, that are more difficult to measure. In other words, it is possible that the various manifestations of inequality are not highly related to one another. In fact, a few scholars, such as Sanday (1974), have analyzed a small number of different dimensions of sex inequality and found that, relative to males, females may be more advantaged in some areas than others. Whyte (1978a, b) examined a "frankly eclectic" set of fifty-two variables, which he assumed tapped the status of women relative to men, in 93 preindustrial cultures. Factor analysis produced nine relatively unrelated dimensions of female status, which led him to conclude that "cross-culturally, there is no such thing as the status of women" (1978a: 214). Some of his dimensions (1978b: 98–100) are not included in this study, some are part of what is here defined as the dependent variable, and some overlap those which constitute independent and intervening variables in this theory.

Given the atheoretical, "grab-bag" set of variables Whyte employed, some of which (as he himself notes, 1978a: 214), do not even appear to directly tap sex inequality (e.g., whether or not there are female initiation ceremonies; remarriage ease), it is premature to conclude, on the basis of this one study, that there is no cross-culturally valid way of comparing the relative status of the sexes. Nevertheless, Whyte's and Sanday's findings alert us to the fact that the numerous manifestations of sex inequality are not necessarily highly correlated. Therefore, the measurement of relative female disadvantage may have to be addressed as an additive phenomenon. For instance, societies may be defined as relatively equalitarian where females are disadvantaged in only a small number of different ways, although the types of disadvantages may differ among them. Conversely, highly sex-stratified societies may be defined as those in which females are disadvantaged on a large number of variables, although again the types of disadvantages may not be the same. Approached in this fashion, a researcher would still need to determine the *extent* of disadvantage on each variable, along with the *number* of disadvantages.

With the exception of Blumberg (1979), explanations of different dimensions of inequality, like explanations of sex inequality in general, to date have tended to focus on societal types or on one type of society only. Much work is needed to develop theories concerning the general variables that impact the degree of equality between the sexes on each separate dimension of inequality. In addition, the relationships between the different dimensions of sexual inequality need more empirical and theoretical exploration. But for this work it will be assumed that it is possible to construct a general, if unrefined, scale of sex inequality consisting of the various dimensions enumerated. The remainder of this book will be an attempt to explain variation in degree of general sex inequality.

It should be noted that the approach to defining sex inequality in this book does not consider the extent to which most members of either or both sexes are "happy" or "contented" or even resigned to their relative status. Women may be highly disadvantaged in a given society yet manifest no displeasure with their status and roles, and may even fail to perceive their relative disadvantage. In this book the perceptual and evaluative components of stratification are ignored. Such issues warrant a separate theory concerning the conditions under which disadvantage is perceived, converted into dissatisfaction, and subsequently into collective action.

Sex Stratification and Social Class

The theory to be presented here treats men and women as internally undifferentiated, general categories. It is clear that in any given society, males and females alike may be sharply differentiated by class, ethnicity, race, and other social stratification variables. A wealthy woman, for instance, is in most ways superior in status and opportunities to a poor man. Nonetheless, it is appropriate to compare the sexes as categories, ignoring other stratification variables, to the extent that women in any given society tend to share approximately the same position *relative to men who are their peers in all ways except sex* (e.g., class, race/ethnicity).

Although this assumption underlies the theory presented here, its use is only heuristic. In class-stratified societies, women in the upper strata are generally more sheltered, i.e., more frequently denied freedom of movement and contact outside the family, than woman in the lower strata. Women in poor families often cannot afford to be absent from economically productive activities. In turn, as will be evident later, such activity contributes heavily to enhancing women's status relative to men's (Blumberg 1979: 128). Thus:

> The status disparity between men and women in the upper class is frequently much greater than among the peasantry and working classes. Notwithstanding stereotypes, and an etiquette of "gallantry" to the contrary, upper class status for a woman is often a gilded cage in which she may share the material comfort and the leisure of the males of her class, but few of the freedoms enjoyed either by lower class women or by male class equals. [Van den Berghe 1973: 98]

In fact, women of high social class (and in modern, industrial, capitalistic societies, often middle-class women as well) may serve the function of symbolizing their male kin's (father's or husband's) social status through conspicuous leisure and conspicuous consumption (Veblen 1953: 229 ff). It is ironic that such a role deprives them of power and status, because the prestige of their male kin depends on their absence from most productive and public roles, rendering them totally dependent on male support for access to societal scarce values. Even where she brings to marriage a substantial amount of her own wealth, quite often that wealth is under the de facto control of male trustees.

Given the fact that social class does have an effect on the relative status of women compared to men, which class should be used to assess the general degree of sex inequality for a total society? One approach is to begin with the assumption that in all human groups, including total societies, the norms and values of those at the top of the stratification hierarchy tend to be imposed upon, accepted by or, at the very least, defined as normatively desirable by the rest of the group. Regardless of the bases of hierarchy (e.g., prestige, race/ethnicity, wealth, age, expertise, force, political power), the degree to which the hierarchy is closed, rigid, or formalized, and the extent of differentiation between the top and the bottom, those on top typically reflect or establish, and attempt to enforce definitions of what is valuable and the rules of the game by which that which is valuable may be obtained.

Given this assumption, one approach to assessing the overall status of women in any given society would be to examine the practices of the highest-status individuals and families in that society. If women are accorded vastly inferior status among the wealthy, powerful, highly prestigious few, than one might assume that women associated with lesser positions along the social stratification hierarchy will tend to be accorded vastly inferior status vis-à-vis those males who are their peers on other stratification dimensions than sex. This approach might tend to exaggerate the extent of female disadvantage. The converse approach would be to examine the status of women relative to men in the lower-classes or strata, on the assumption that they constitute the majority, if not the overwhelming bulk, of the population in class-stratified societies. Although numerically a more representative segment of the female population, this measurement procedure might tend to underestimate, at least slightly, the relative disadvantages faced by women in such societies.

Two other options exist for measuring the relative status of women in class-stratified societies. First, one could examine the status of middle-class women vis-à-vis their male counterparts. This group is simultaneously freed from the financial necessity to engage in productive labor (unlike their class inferiors) and less remote from the everyday life of societal members than the females of socially elite families. But when one considers the full range of class-stratified societies, the relative size of an entity that might be termed "middle class" varies so extensively, from a few percent in many agrarian societies to as much as half in postindustrial, that between-society comparability is jeopardized. Finally, some sort of weighted average that takes into account the distribution of population by class/strata could be computed. While this would constitute the most valid measure, in practical terms it might prove very difficult.

In short, within class-stratified societies, women's status relative to men is not a constant (a phenomenon possibly compounded in multiethnic/racial/religious societies). But regardless of the measurement technique employed to operationalize the degree of sex inequality as a dependent variable, for heuristic purposes it can and will be assumed that such a single measure does make sense conceptually. Stated other-wise, between-class variance in the status of women relative to their male class peers is probably minimal compared to between-society variance in the overall status of women compared to men.

Overview of a Theory of Sex Stratification

The theory to be developed in this book is represented schematically in Figure 1.2. In later chapters the primary direction of influence between interacting variables will be distinguished from feedback relationships, which distinction, for purposes of simplification, does not appear on this chart. In the remainder of this chapter, each variable will be defined conceptually, and the major linkages, that is, the central logic of the theory, will be discussed.

THE THEORETICAL VARIABLES

The dependent variable *Degree of Sex Stratification* has already been defined. The following will define the additional variables in Figure 1.2 from right to left, i.e., from intervening to independent variables.

2. *Degree of Gender Differentiation.* Societies differ on the extent and degree to which males and females are expected to differ (regardless of whether or not they actually do), on traits of behavior, personality, interests, and intellect. Gender stereotypes have been loosely placed together under the rubric "gender roles" which, while probably a misnomer (see Chafetz 1978: chap. 1; 1980b), is a conventional and convenient term. It is important to note, however, that the variable "gender differentiation" does not include specific social roles assigned to men and women (e.g., particular work or familial roles). Social roles, as contrasted with general expectations concerning behavior and psychic and intellectual traits, are treated in terms of other variables in this theory. It would therefore be tautological to include them in this variable.

In all known societies adult males and females confront different social expectations concerning their personal behavior and characteristics. Cross-culturally, wide variation exists in definitions of appropriate mas-culine and feminine traits and behaviors, with particular traits defined as masculine in one society and feminine in another, or as the province of neither or both sexes (see Mead 1935 for examples). Moreover, and more important in this context, societies differ in the degree to which gender differentiation exists, a variable rarely treated in the current literature on gender roles and sex stratification. At one extreme a society may assume very few categorical differences between the sexes, for

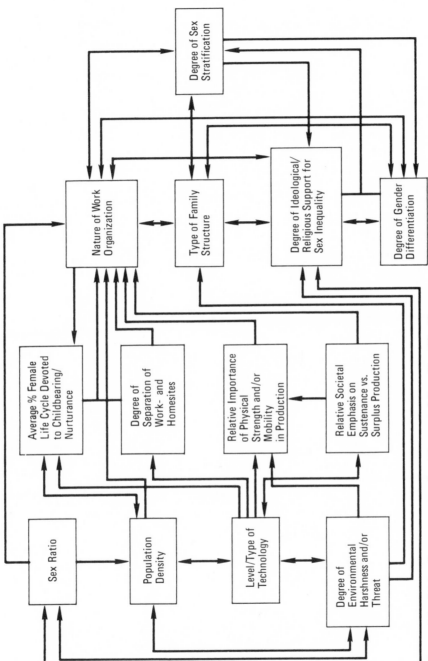

Figure 1.2 Main Components of a Theory of Sex Stratification

example, the Arapesh studied by Mead (1935), while at the other extreme the sexes are considered "opposite" one another, as in Victorian England.

Measurement of gender differentiation is, in fact, measurement of stereotypes, not necessarily of real behavior (see Chafetz 1980b); and while precise information is lacking for many, if not most, cultures, the methodology is available to measure this variable with considerable precision. The same type of approach used to measure racial stereotypes could be employed in modified form to measure gender differentiation. It is important to note that the concept "gender differentiation" does not imply inequality. It is logically possible to talk about "separate [different] but equal." Empirically, it appears that "different" is strongly associated with unequal; that is, degree of gender differentiation and degree of sex stratification are highly correlated (Sanday 1974). Conceptually, however, they are distinct variables. In this theory, degree of gender differentiation serves as an intervening variable, which is affected by the degree of sex stratification, but which in turn affects it primarily in interaction with, or through the influence of other variables which it directly affects.

3. *Degree of Ideological/Religious Support for Sex Inequality.* Societies differ in the extent to which dominant religious and/or secular ideologies explicitly support extensive gender differentiation and sex stratification. Virtually all of the world's great religious systems (Christianity, Judaism, Islam, Hinduism, Buddhism) explicitly support a system of sexual inequality and substantial gender differentiation, although there are differences in degree among them and within many of them according to denominational distinctions. The reason for this support lies in the types of societies in which they originally arose, and will be discussed later in this book. Not all societies, however, are or have been dominated by one of these world religions.

Many societies today have secular, often political ideologies that explicitly support sex equality and, sometimes, a minimum of gender differentiation. Such ideologies are often codified in a constitution and/or other legal statements of the society, which state the rights, obligations, and prescribed and prohibited behaviors of citizens. These secular ideologies may sometimes contradict dominant religious views pertaining to sex and gender. At any rate, societies differ widely in the degree to which their ideologies support sex equality, and this theory suggests a direct effect of ideology, in conjunction with the gender differentiation variable, on degree of sex stratification, as well as a feedback mechanism tending to reinforce the dominant religious and/or secular ideology.

4. *Nature of Work Organization.* As will become apparent, the way in which a society structures or organizes its productive activities is the

single, most important set of variables in this theory. This intervening variable is a composite of six variables.

The first, the division of labor by sex, concerns societal definitions of men's work versus women's work. Definitions of sex-appropriate work differ substantially from society to society. In this instance, however, the specific tasks are less important than two other features of labor division. First, in societies which produce little or no surplus, the extent of the contribution of each sex to acquiring or producing basic sustenance is important. Second, in societies which produce a surplus, the extent to which the activities of each sex contribute to that surplus—the exchange goods—is important. Exchange (surplus) production is typically more highly valued everywhere than sustenance production (Nielsen 1978: 19), probably because surplus goods can be exchanged outside the family to create non-kin networks of mutual obligations. Such obligations, in turn, can provide the basis for both prestige and power (see Friedl 1975). Therefore, the extent to which females contribute to the most highly valued productive activities of their societies constitutes the first work organization variable.

A second dimension of the work organization variable concerns the extent to which the work typically done by members of each sex is easily replaceable by members of the other sex, or unemployed members of one's own sex (see Blumberg 1978: 28). If one sex does work that the other could readily do, usually because of the low skill-level involved, then regardless of the inherent importance of the task(s) for the group, little value tends to be attached to the work. In general, workers who perform tasks that many others can do tend to receive relatively few scarce and valued resources in return for their work.

If these two aspects of work organization are combined, sex inequality will tend to be greatest where (a) women produce relatively few sustenance products in a nonexchange economy, (b) women produce relatively few surplus products in an exchange economy, (c) in either economy, women's work is of low skill-level hence readily replaceable, or (d) at whatever skill level, a surplus of potential workers exists capable of doing the same work done by female producers.

Another dimension of work organization important to explaining degree of sex stratification refers to the extent to which the productive roles in a society are sex-segregated. Here the issue is not focused on the relative contributions of each sex to surplus vs. sustenance production; rather, the important issue is the extent to which males and females specialize in very different forms of work activity. For instance, in hunting/gathering societies, male hunters may receive more prestige than female gatherers, despite the fact that the latter may contribute more to sustenance and that both are engaged in sustenance production,

14

DEFINING THE ISSUES

because of the scarcity, hence high value, of animal protein. In industrial
societies, all else being equal (e.g., educational and skill requirements),
occupations that are female-dominated typically receive less income and
often less prestige than those that are not (see Berch 1982: 81; Chafetz
1972; Glenn and Feldberg 1982). It is unclear whether the presence of
a high proportion of females in a particular occupation serves to suppress
income and possibly prestige, or whether the relatively low pay and
prestige of such occupations serve to keep males from selecting the
occupation, when they can choose instead from a range of alternatives
not available to most females. Recent research in the United States
(Almquist 1977; Bergmann and Adelman 1973; Featherman and Hauser
1976: 463; Ferber and Lowry 1976) suggests that sex segregation of jobs,
especially entry-level positions, accounts for more of the difference in
male and female incomes than other variables, such as education or
experience.

The fourth dimension of the work organization variable pertains to
the attention span required for various production activities (see Blumberg
1979: 122). People who are involved in the care of young children (and
they are almost universally women) cannot readily perform tasks that
require lengthy attention spans, since their work is likely to be interrupted
frequently by their offspring. Therefore, the degree to which women
are involved in production activities and the extent to which activities
are sex-segregated will depend in part on the attention span required
to do the kinds of work that characterize a particular society.

The final two components of the composite work organization variable,
which are highly interrelated, involve the ownership or, more important,
control of the means (land and capital) and the products (including
salaries or wages in money-based societies) of production. In societies
where labor involves sustenance production only, the degree to which
women control the distribution of the products (mostly food) their labor
produces will strongly influence their relative status. The means of
production are typically simple (e.g., a stick, a container) and accessible
to all. The ability to grant or withhold the product, namely, the necessities
of life, will therefore tend to influence strongly the relative status of
each sex. Where surplus production is developed, those who profit will
be those who can choose the manner in which the surplus will be
distributed, the product owners. The means of production involved in
surplus production are often elaborate and/or scarce (e.g., privately
owned land, expensive machinery). Those who are able to control the
means of production will also tend to be able to control the product,
whether or not their labor is involved in production (Nielsen 1978: 39).
Thus, to the extent that the economic (and, as will be discussed later,
the family) organization places control of the means and/or products

of production disproportionately in the hands of men, women's status will tend to be very low, while it will tend to approach equality where women control the means and the products of their labor. Control over work products can mitigate the effects of the division of labor. Specifically, even if women produce most of the goods, if they do not also control their distribution, women's relative status will tend to be low (see Blumberg 1978, chap. 3; Van den Berghe 1973: 72). Of course, the same principle applies in terms of other stratification variables. As Lenski (1966) demonstrated, social class inequality arises only when societies produce a surplus. Expropriation of surplus, i.e., control over the distribution of surplus products, is the root of all structured inequality, sexual as well as class.

5. *Type of Family Structure.* The composite variable *Nature of Work Organization* and the variable *Type of Family Structure* constitute the most important intervening variables in this theory. The second also is a composite and is comprised of three separate variables.

The first two components of family structure of relevance to this theory are lineality and locality. Lineality refers to the descent line and can be roughly divided into matrilineal, patrilineal, and bilateral. Lineage will directly affect which, if either, sex tends to monopolize the ownership of the means and products of production. Locality refers to the residence choice of families. Families may live with or near the husband's kin (patrilocal), the wife's kin (matrilocal), or may set up an independent residence (neolocal). In turn, locality and lineage tend to be associated with one another.

As a general proposition, it is safe to assert that women's relative status tends to be highest in cases of matrilineality and matrilocality (Blumberg 1978: 43–44; Martin and Voorhies 1975: 224–25; Schlegel 1972: 98, 101–2), and very low in cases of patrilineality and patrilocality (Nielsen 1978: 30). For instance, under patrilineality women's sexuality is often severely controlled relative to the control exercised over men's sexual behavior. Restricting women's sexuality to marriage ensures known and "proper" paternity, which is necessary to patrilineage. Moreover, restrictions on women's sexuality are closely related to restrictions on their physical movements in public, which are designed to further ensure premarital virginity and marital faithfulness. In general, it appears that the more women are involved in the important productive activities of their society, and the more they control the products of their labor, the less likely the family structure is to be patrilineal and patrilocal. Other formal aspects of family structure, such as the institutions of bride price and dowry, and polygyny/monogamy, may be related to the status of women, but they are not central to explaining it. Indeed, they are probably better viewed as partial indicators of women's relative status, and are thus omitted from the family structure variable.

The third dimension of family structure of importance in this theory concerns the division of household labor. The literature concerning gender roles and sex inequality often makes two closely related types of distinctions relevant here. On the one hand, productive activity is separated conceptually from reproductive activity. The latter is taken to refer not only to the biological act of reproduction, but to the nurturing and socialization of children and to the related duties (e.g., food preparation, care of domicile) that accompany what Engels (1968) viewed as the reproduction of the labor force. The second common distinction concerns "public sphere vs. private sphere" ("domestic") activities (see O'Kelly 1980, chap. 2; Rosaldo 1974). "Public sphere" refers to production for exchange purposes and societal decision-making and ritual activities; "private sphere," to the reproductive, consumptive, and related domestic or maintenance activities, including the production of goods for use value. Substantial consensus exists that the more the sexes specialize in one or the other of these activity clusters (that is, that males specialize in the productive/public sphere, females in the reproductive/private sphere), the greater the sex inequality. Stated differently, the more the tasks associated with the maintenance of the household, including childcare, are divided equally by sex (i.e., the less the household division of labor), the less the sex inequality. While nowhere do males specialize in the reproductive/private sphere activities, societies can and do vary from near-equality in the division of household tasks to total female specialization, that is, virtual absence of males from participation in such tasks. It is likely that where males contribute little or nothing to household tasks, they tend to monopolize the bulk of the productive/public sphere tasks, and vice versa.

6. *Relative Importance of Physical Strength and/or Mobility in Production.* Individual females may be stronger than individual males, but as categories males are physically stronger than females. While female endurance is somewhat greater than male, females encumbered by pregnancy and/or care of very young children tend to be less capable of regular, sustained, and rapid physical mobility than males. Therefore, if a form of production requires great physical strength (e.g., early plow agriculture) or far-ranging mobility (most forms of large-game hunting, many forms of pastoral activities), females will tend to be absent from them (see Blumberg 1978: 26). Females who do participate in them are less likely to produce offspring who survive to maturity than do other females because of higher miscarriage rates, greater threat to their lives, and greater threat to the lives of their dependent youngsters. Thus, over a few generations the practice of female participation should decline as

nonparticipating women rear daughters trained as nonparticipants, and as participating females are less successful in rearing daughters who survive to reproduce. Therefore, the more physical strength and/or physical mobility are characteristic of the primary productive activities of a society, the more females will be absent from the productive activities of their society, with the result that the degree of sexual inequality will be high.

7. *Average Percentage of Female Life Cycle Devoted to Childbearing/ Child Nurturance.* Societies differ in the average number of pregnancies women experience and in the amount of time during which women are bound to the care of very young children, although the "breeder-feeder" roles are reserved for women in all societies (Boulding 1976). At one extreme are the societies in which women are frequently pregnant and/ or nursing children who cannot be left for long by the mother. Traditional agrarian societies often exemplify this extreme. At the other end of the continuum, such as typified by modern industrial societies, women average few children and wean them early or bottle-feed them. This allows mothers to leave children in the care of others. In a society with a high birthrate, women devote the major segment of their life spans to the care of their own children, except where the infant mortality rate is also extremely high. Where the birthrate is low, a few adults (almost always women) can take care of the children of many women, allowing the mothers to spend the bulk of their adult years in productive labor. And the longer the life expectancy of women, the more years they will have after child-rearing to engage in productive labor, regardless of family size. Historically, however, higher birthrates are usually associated with lower female life expectancy, as constant pregnancy strains women's health and helps to age them prematurely. Moreover, for most of human history childbirth deaths were frequent and, therefore, the more a woman's pregnancies, the more times she was at risk of dying prematurely.

8. *Degree of Separation of Work- and Homesites.* Societies also differ on the extent to which worksites are separated physically from homesites. At one extreme—in simple horticultural societies, for example—the work-site may be contiguous with the residence. At the other extreme, many miles may separate the two, such as in modern industrial societies. To the extent that women are pregnant and/or nursing mothers, it is difficult for them to work efficiently long distances from their domicile, and women as a category will be curtailed in their productive efforts by their maternal responsibilities. Moreover, as stated earlier, women who travel great distances from their homes, either leaving their young children or taking them along, are less likely than other women to have children who survive to reproduce. Therefore, the greater the distance between worksite and home *and* the greater the average number of pregnancies

and/or breast-feeding children, the less involved women as a group will tend to be in productive activities (see Blumberg 1978: 26). To the extent that they are less involved in production, they will tend to suffer from curtailed access to the scarce and valued resources of their society.

9. *Relative Societal Emphasis on Sustenance vs. Surplus Production.* When the variable *Nature of Work Organization* was discussed, it was pointed out that in societies that produce a surplus, production of exchange commodities is usually more highly valued than production of sustenance commodities. The potential of a collectivity for producing an economic surplus is, in large measure, a function of its technology (Lenski 1966). According to Lenski's general schema, hunting/gathering societies lack the technological capacity to produce a surplus, horticultural societies may be able to produce a small surplus, agricultural societies can produce a larger one, and industrial societies produce still more. But being technically able to produce surplus goods does not automatically mean that a society will do so. At least among horticultural societies, some "take life easy" and produce only that which is necessary to survive. Sahlins (1972, chap. 1) suggests that even hunting/gathering societies may produce little because they desire little, rather than because they are incapable of producing more. Other societies, however, work harder and produce a surplus (Blumberg 1978: 14, 35). The reasons for such differences in cultural values pertaining to productivity vs. leisure are under debate. One possible reason is that in societies where the level of external threat is high, people perceive a need to establish networks of mutual obligation with non-kin. Such networks can be established by giving gifts to non-kin, which will elicit a reciprocity norm. Thus, a desire to produce a surplus is, in fact, a desire to create an exchangeable commodity for building alliances (suggested by Desley Deacon, personal communication).

Regardless of why they do so, the fact that some societies pursue surplus production does have implications for work organization, family structure and, consequently, degree of sex stratification. More than a century ago, Engels (1968: 495) concluded that as the wealth of a community increased, lineage patterns shifted from female- to male-dominated (i.e., from matrilineal to patrilineal), which, as mentioned earlier, is associated with heightened sex inequality (see also Martin and Voorhies 1975: 233 ff; Schlegel 1972: 80). In general, increased surplus production requires more substantial involvement of males in production than is true in societies that produce only for sustenance. In turn, greater male productive involvement entails direct effects on both the nature of work organization and the family structure, hence the degree of sex stratification.

10. *Level and Type of Technology.* The level/type of technology available to a society does not stand in linear relationship to the other variables

in this theory. For instance, some developments that are generally considered more advanced (e.g., the replacement of the hoe by the plow) actually require greater human strength and effort than simpler technologies. In these cases technological development may serve to decrease women's economic contributions and relative status. Other technological developments, such as industrialization, can have the opposite impact. The technology available to a society impacts the location of worksite relative to homesite (by affecting transportation or the need to coordinate work roles), the amount of physical mobility and/or strength required for productive activities, the birthrate (birth control technology), and the amount of surplus a society is capable of producing, all of which, in turn, have indirect effects, via their impact on the work organization variables, on the degree of sex stratification, as they sometimes improve, sometimes decrease, the status of women relative to men. More important, it is likely that technological level and type are indirectly but powerfully responsible for the shape of most major social institutions, and it is thus very likely that changes in family structure, work organization, and ultimately the system of sex stratification are often, if not usually, rooted in technological change.

11. *Degree of Environmental Harshness and/or Threat.* This variable consists of two components. First, there is the physical environment: what level of exertion is required for a group to "subsist" in a given environmental niche? It is clear that as technology advances, difficult environments become less onerous, but this variable must be included, at least when one considers technologically simple societies. For instance, it is more difficult for a group without sophisticated technology to survive in the tundra or desert than in temperate climates and moderately vegetated terrains. The second component of this definition refers to the social environment: the extent to which a group is threatened by other groups of people.

In cases of a harsh physical environment, the search for food may entail extensive travel from the homesite. While groups tend to be nomadic in such environments (e.g., the Bedouin), there is nonetheless a premium on unfettered, rapid mobility in pursuit of game or grazing lands. Males, who as discussed earlier have greater general mobility, tend to monopolize the major productive activities, which, in turn, serves to increase the status differences between males and females (Martin and Voorhies 1975: 341). Physical or social situations that make group survival difficult or problematic seem to promote male cohesiveness (Martin and Voorhies 1975: 222–23, 234). Patrilineality and patrilocality enhance male group solidarity (Nielsen 1978: 30). Males tied together by blood kinship and lifelong acquaintance typically work together more cooperatively and with less competition and hostility than non-kin males. Whether for the purpose of waging war (overwhelmingly a male task) or doing strenuous labor to gain sustenance or produce a surplus, cohesive male groups, hence patrilineality, patrilocality, and a relatively low status for women, seem to be a frequent result (Martin and Voorhies 1975: 223).

12. *Sex Ratio.* The sex ratio of a society is the total number of males divided by the total number of females and standardized to a base of 100. A ratio in excess of 100 means more males than females in the population; under 100 is the opposite. It might seem self-evident that societal (or community) sex ratios should all be about 100, give or take a bit, except possibly when war thins out the male population. Guttentag and Secord (1983) have demonstrated, however, that this is not the case. Orthodox Jews, for instance, have sex ratios approaching 150—at birth; American blacks today have a sex ratio in the low 90s. The reasons for such skewed sex ratios are many, and only a few concern us here. A skewed sex ratio may reflect a different value placed on each sex, by which one sex gets fed first and most, receives better medical attention, etc. It may also reflect a practice of infanticide based on sex. These practices are not unusual, especially where population pressure and food shortages exist. They typically reflect higher status for males, meaning that female children receive less food, female infants are killed, etc. In turn, the resulting dearth of females will help to reduce future population growth. More important, where a high sex ratio exists (i.e., a surplus of males), the relative status of women is often enhanced (Guttentag and Secord 1983). Their scarcity makes them more valuable, both as workers, since they are less replaceable, and as marriage partners, since there aren't enough to go around (e.g., the frontier West in 19th-century America).

13. *Population Density.* Population density refers to the number of people in a society, given the available resources necessary to sustain them. A sophisticated technology or a lush environment can support more people than a harsh environment or a simpler technology. Therefore, population density is not simply the number of people per some unit of space. Moreover, the absolute number of people may make an environment harsh that could have sustained fewer people easily. Population pressure (i.e., high density) may be a force spurring technological development; it may affect the societal ability to produce a surplus; it may make some part of the work force more replaceable; it may even create chronic wars between neighboring societies. Finally, as suggested previously, it may function to alter the sex ratio by encouraging female infanticide or the withholding of scarce resources, such as food, from females. In any and all of these ways it will have an indirect effect on degree of sex stratification.

It should be apparent, both from this brief discussion of the variables included in the theory and from Figure 1.2, that what is being proposed is an open-systems model of sex stratification. Undoubtedly, other, unspecified variables influence those included, thus affecting the dependent variable, if only indirectly. Moreover, it must be understood that each of the specified variables impacts each other variable, if only indirectly through some third, fourth, or N^{th} variable. Thus, change in any one variable has some impact on all other variables, including, of course, the degree of sex stratification. Based on the existing literature I believe that this model includes all variables with a significant impact on degree of sex stratification and all of the important linkages between these variables. In statistical terminology, it is postulated that the variables specified will collectively account for most of the variance in the dependent variable when the theory is systematically tested. Finally, the model presented in this book is also macro-structural, (c.f., Mayhew 1980); that is, there are no psychological or individual-level variables included; the variables all pertain to properties of total societies.

Why Can't Women Be Superior to Men?

As was apparent in Figure 1.1, the empirical variation in degree of sex stratification requiring explanation ranges from near-equality to virtually total male advantage. Using the variables just discussed, it is possible to speculate why the logically possible half of the continuum that encompasses greater female advantage is nowhere to be found.

The central thesis of this theory is simple: the degree of sex stratification is a direct function of the extent to which the organization of production permits women to contribute to the production of valued resources and to control the output of such production. The family structure is both influenced by and, in turn, helps to shape the organization of production. Therefore, family structure also strongly affects women's status relative to men's. These two interrelated, intervening sets of variables are impacted by a series of demographic, technical, and environmental phenomena. In turn, they affect social definitional variables that serve to buttress further the existing sex stratification system.

To answer the question "Why are women nowhere superior to men in their access to scarce and valued societal resources?" one must look to the key sets of intervening variables. As a category, men nowhere specialize solely in the reproductive/private sphere activities, nor do women as a group specialize solely in the productive/public sphere. Stated otherwise, women's activities are either specialized in nonproductive roles, which leads to inferior status, or divided between the two realms, which may afford them relatively equal status.

This pushes the quest back one step: why do women as a category never specialize solely in productive/public sector roles? Since this is a constant, logically it must be explained in terms of one or more constants. In this case, a set of biological constants helps to answer the question raised (see Blumberg 1978: 26): the women carry babies in their bodies and lactate, which circumscribes their physical mobility. While this can be minimized through low birthrates and bottle feeding, it cannot be eliminated and, in fact, for most human societies throughout most of human history, such restriction due to pregnancy and nursing has been far from minimal. Given these biological facts, most societies find it more efficient if women also do the bulk of the caretaking of young children who are no longer nursing. That is, on the basis of expediency, the nurturance role is typically extended beyond the biologically based phenomenon of breast-feeding. And to the extent that these factors keep women in the proximity of the domicile more than men, it becomes more efficient to extend their domestic role to encompass other household tasks, such as food preparation and maintenance of family possessions. Since many societies have had a large share of their productive activities moved away from the homesite, these fetters on female mobility restrict women's opportunity to specialize in productive roles.

An additional biological constant is probably in force: male superiority in physical strength. In many societies, especially preindustrial, some or many productive activities require—or at least are handled more efficiently by—greater strength. Again, females as a category find themselves somewhat disadvantaged in competing for such roles.

In short, females are not found to have superior status to males because their relative disadvantage in mobility and/or strength makes it more efficient for men to monopolize some, many, or all productive roles and for women to assume at least some of the household labor. Thus, women as a category are never free to specialize in or monopolize productive/public sector roles. Where men do specialize in and monopolize such roles, they are vastly superior to women in status. Where the sexes more equally divide the two realms, their statuses approach equality. Females as a group cannot have vastly superior status to males inasmuch as, in all the history of our species, they have never been able to divest themselves of some involvement in the reproductive/ private sphere of activity.

In the remainder of this book the linkages between the variables defined in this chapter will be examined in more detail, using exemplary material from a large array of different types of societies, and the theory presented diagramatically in this chapter will be presented as a series of propositions.

2

THE SOCIAL DEFINITIONAL
VARIABLES

The model reviewed briefly in Chapter 1 includes two variables that refer to societal definitions relevant to sex and gender: degree of gender differentiation and degree of ideological/religious support for sex inequality. These are the only variables in the theory which refer directly to social psychological phenomena. Yet they, like all other variables in the theory, are considered at the macro or societal level, not at the individual or micro-level.

Structural variables alone can never fully explain human behavior. Despite the fact that the dependent variable *Degree of Sex Stratification* is a social structural, rather than an individual behavioral variable, it nonetheless is rooted in, that is, emerges from, the behavior of a large number of individuals in any given society. *The patterned regularity of people's behavior comes to comprise structure.* The degree of sex stratification is, in reality, an emergent property that arises out of the ways in which members (not, of course, all) of both sexes treat each other. If it is said that one sex is highly disadvantaged relative to the other, it is a shorthand way of noting that in tens of thousands, even millions of concrete interactive instances, individuals of the more-advantaged sex are able to control the behavior of individuals of the less-advantaged sex, and to withhold and/or extract from them goods, services, compliance, deference, opportunities, etc. In short, in the final analysis structure arises from countless individuals behaving in certain patterned ways, although substantial variation at the individual level does exist.

To say that structural variables arise from recurrent individual behavior implies that certain recurrent, patterned mental processes also occur. That is, much if not most human behavior is motivated and/or justified by attitudes, beliefs, values, i.e., mental processes. To the extent that a set of behaviors is patterned, regular, predictable, it can be assumed that the attitudes, beliefs, values which motivate, justify, and/or give meaning to that behavioral set are also patterned, regular, predictable. The two variables to be discussed in this chapter refer precisely to such patterned mental processes. More precisely, they refer to the degree to which societies are characterized by patterns of thought (beliefs, values, attitudes) referring to sex and gender—the extent to which the individual members of a society and/or some powerful elite(s) tend to share similar definitions concerning sex and gender, however these arise initially or are learned individually.

Degree of Gender Differentiation

Recall from Chapter 1 that the variable *gender differentiation* refers to the extent to which societies (that is, societal members) expect males and females, on the sole basis of their categorical membership, to manifest different traits of behavior, personality, intellect, and interest, regardless of whether they in fact do so. Societies with a low level of gender differentiation would be characterized by the fact that their members hold few expectations that people would vary on these kinds of traits on the basis of sex alone; those with high levels of gender differentiation would be characterized by the fact that their members expect wide variation on the basis of sex alone. Stated in another way, gender differentiation refers to the extent to which societies develop sex-based stereotypes (see Chafetz 1980b). A stereotype is a belief that individuals who share one characteristic (in this case the same sex) will exhibit a series of other traits common to them but different from those not sharing that characteristic (i.e., members of the other sex). Stereotypes are social, not merely individual, phenomena; they tend to be widely known and accepted by members of a society. Of course, the extent to which sex stereotypes are widely known and accepted by societal members is one good indicator of degree of gender differentiation.

The variable *Degree of Gender Differentiation* is not, to my knowledge, to be found in the published literature concerning gender roles. Scholars interested in gender roles typically look at the content of the masculine and feminine roles of a given society and/or the degree to which one role is defined in more negative terms than the other (see Chafetz 1978, chap. 2). To the limited extent that cross-cultural or historical work exists concerning gender roles, it focuses on a comparison of societies or time periods in terms of the contents of each role. For instance, societies might be compared to see to what extent one or more traits defined as feminine in society X at time 1 are also defined as feminine

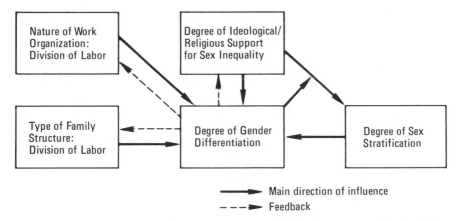

Figure 2.1   Direct Theoretical Linkages of *Degree of Gender Differentiation*
to Other Variables

elsewhere and/or at other times. By contrast, the concern here is not
with content, which is totally ignored, but with degree of difference
between the ways in which each gender is stereotypically defined,
regardless of what traits are assigned to each. It is important to recall
that to define the sexes as different does not automatically mean that
they are unequal (although the minorities literature suggests that this
relationship exists, e.g., see Dworkin 1970). If gender differentiation
logically implied sexual inequality, it would be tautological to include
the former in a theory purporting to explain the latter. The two variables
are, however, logically independent of one another. In the minorities
literature, the study of stereotypes typically includes, at least implicitly,
concern with status differences and thus with the extent of prejudice
and/or discrimination. Here, invidious distinctions are left to other
variables, and attention is focused solely on the extent of difference in
defining the two sex aggregates.

   Figure 2.1 shows all direct linkages of other variables in the theory
to *Degree of Gender Differentiation*. The postulated main direction of
influence is indicated by a solid line, secondary or feedback relationships
by a dashed line. A solid line with arrows going in both directions
depicts approximately equal impact of the variables upon one another.
(These symbols will be used in all subsequent figures throughout the
book.) Recall also that this is a systems model, meaning that the other
variables in the theory are all indirectly linked to this one as well,
which will also pertain throughout the remainder of this book.

GENDER DIFFERENTIATION AND ROLE SPECIALIZATION

Psychologists and social psychologists, including most specialists in the area of gender roles, have tended to depict gender traits as relatively stable traits of personality and intellect learned during early childhood socialization and reinforced by a variety of social and interpersonal mechanisms throughout life (see Chafetz 1978, esp. chap. 3, for a review of the pertinent literature). From this perspective, extensive gender differentiation would be linked to different socialization practices directed at boys and girls, eventuating in real differences in personality and intellectual traits of adult men and women. In turn, such real differences in intellect and personality would presumably affect the abilities of members of each gender to function in concrete roles in both the public/ productive and private/reproductive spheres. Playing different social roles in the economy and family, in turn, would result in differential access to societal scarce and valued resources, that is, the degree of sex stratification. The copious popular and professional literature (and action programs) in this country directed at "remediating" females—their math anxiety, their lack of assertiveness, their unwillingness to accept job-related responsibility—testifies to this perspective. Presumably, American women are disadvantaged in attaining higher prestige and higher paying jobs because they lack traits socialized into males from childhood and deemed important to functioning in most high-status work roles (see Chafetz 1978: 53–54).

This approach is predicated on two debatable assumptions. First, it assumes that most real flesh-and-blood people in fact have traits concordant with the gender stereotypes. In other words, it reifies the stereotypes. Second, it assumes stability of traits: that traits are learned during childhood (if not innate to each sex) and tend to remain with the individual throughout life unless specifically combated through conscious means.

In terms of the first assumption, more than a decade of psychological research casts serious doubt on the extent to which most Americans exhibit traits concordant with American gender stereotypes. Research on the "fear of success," originally conceived as a female "problem" (Horner 1968), has often shown males to suffer equally or even more from it, depending on the situation described in measuring it (see Cherry and Deaux 1975; Garske 1975; and for a summary of this research, Schaffer 1981: 63–65). Research utilizing the Bem Sex Role Inventory (BSRI) has shown a remarkable richness and complexity in supposed gender traits once they were reconceptualized into two scales, one each for masculinity and femininity, with different forms of combinations and permutations. Many Americans score low on both, high on both, or as "masculine" females or "feminine" males (see Bem 1976; Spence and Helmrich 1978). For instance, in a study of students Bem (1977) found that only about half were "appropriately" sex-typed, while 35 percent were "androgynous," and 15 percent were "cross" sex-typed. In their general review of the sex-role literature, Maccoby and Jacklin (1974) found relatively few traits that can confidently be said to be clearly associated with sex, and most differences that do exist between the sexes are small, meaning that empirically there is substantial overlap between males and females. It is clear that gender stereotypes cannot be assumed accurately to describe most males and females in any society.

In terms of the second assumption, Nielsen has suggested that people's behavior is primarily a function not of deep-seated traits of personality, but of situational phenomena. From this perspective, one acts nurturant not primarily because of a trait of nurturance learned early in life (or innate), but because of the requirements associated with a primary parental role; one acts competitively not because one *is* competitive, but because of the role requirements of a job in a competitive setting. Nielsen (1978: 120–21) concludes: "Although socialization and its effects may set outer limits to behavior, the social role being played may dictate which learned behaviors are expressed at any given time." Kanter's research on the behavior of male and female corporate managers leads to the same conclusions (1976, 1977). She finds that structural variables associated with a position—degree of power, number of people similar in social characteristics, and opportunity to advance—are associated with work-related behavior and attitudes, not sex or gender per se. Where men and women managers are similar in terms of their opportunities to advance, their power, and in not being "tokens," they behave similarly. That the sexes are rarely similar in these three ways (nor are the races) accounts for the obvious ways in which their behavior may differ.

The point here is that to the extent that women and men perform different roles in productive and/or familial contexts, they are likely to behaviorly express different traits of personality and intellect. These traits are malleable, however; they change (within limits) according to situational change. Conversely, to the extent that males and females play similar roles, their traits tend to be similar. For instance, American black females, regardless of marital status, expect and are expected to work in economically productive roles far more than their white counterparts (at least until very recently). Traditionally, black men and women also have had less-stereotyped gender roles than their white counterparts (see Ladner 1972; Yorburg 1974). Where men and women have similar parenting roles (e.g., the Arapesh studied by Mead, 1935), both are viewed as fundamentally nurturant. Likewise, among the Semang and

Lepcha, men and women perform similar roles and there is little differentiation in gender attributes (Sanday 1981: 19–21; 83–84).

In Figure 2.1, these points are indicated by the solid lines linking family structure, on one hand, and nature of work organization, on the other hand, to degree of gender differentiation. Stated propositionally:

2.1. *The more differentiated (specialized or segregated) the division of labor in the family, the greater the degree of gender differentiation, and vice versa.*

2.2. *The more differentiated (specialized or segregated) the division of productive labor, the greater the degree of gender differentiation, and vice versa.*

The argument just presented implies that role differentiation (specialization or segregation) tends to create *real* differences in behavior among males and females. Earlier it was argued that gender stereotypes may not be matched by real differences between the two sexes. These two statements are not contradictory. First, to say that such stereotypes *may not describe* reality accurately does not mean they *never* do so. Second, and more important, the argument claims that people's *behavior* reflects their roles. In reality, their inner traits may or may not be congruent with their behavior. Especially, they may have traits which they have no opportunity to express. Regardless of any consideration of deep-seated inner traits, the more different the social roles performed by each sex, the more different their general behavior, and this in turn creates the wide-spread perception, i.e., stereotypes, that the sexes are indeed fundamentally different. Conversely, the more similar their roles, hence general behavior, the less there will be societal-wide stereotyping of the sexes. Restated in terms of the full logic, then, the propositions might read:

2.3. *The more differentiated (specialized or segregated) the division of labor in the family and/or the division of productive labor, the more the sexes tend to be distinguished by general behavioral differences, and vice versa.*

2.4. *The more the sexes are distinguished by general behavioral differences, the greater the degree of gender differentiation tends to be (i.e., perceptions or stereotypes of fundamental gender differences), and vice versa.*

If stereotypes arise from role differentiation, in turn they reinforce such role differentiation, as indicated by the term "and vice versa" in the propositions presented. Group stereotypes typically consist of both positively and negatively valued traits (although they may not be equal in number or relative importance). Each sex is thought to be better equipped for some purposes or in some ways than the other, worse for other purposes or in other ways (see Chafetz 1978, chap. 2). This evaluative component is actually a matter of prejudice, which typically accompanies stereotyping. To the extent that each sex is perceived as better suited for certain roles than others, mechanisms ranging from socialization practices (e.g., different types of toys for girls and boys), to counseling, informal job discrimination, and legal restrictions and obligations, will serve to channel most males and females into what are defined as "appropriate" roles in the family and the economy (productive sphere). Thus, feedback arrows appear on Figure 2.1 showing that the degree of gender differentiation impacts family structure and work organization. For example, until the last decade many states legally barred American females from jobs that involved lifting "heavy" objects (in at least one case defined as low as 40 pounds). Stereotypically, women have been seen as the "weaker sex." Men, on the other hand, were legally responsible for the economic support of their families, which essentially barred them from full-time home-making (Kanowitz 1969). In Westernized societies throughout most of this century, the prevalent stereotype that women are "naturally" destined to be mothers and that mothers ought to be home with their children led to restrictions on married women's employment. For instance, American communities often barred married women from teaching earlier in the century. The Australian civil service, the largest single employer in that nation, barred married women from employment from its inception in 1902 until 1966 (Deacon 1982).

In summary, the division of labor, both within the domestic/reproductive sphere and the public/productive sphere, shapes societal perceptions of "appropriate" masculine and feminine traits. These perceptions, or stereotypes, in turn typically buttress the existing patterns of labor division. It is clear that changes in labor division and/or gender stereotypes can and do occur; and if either changes in any given society, for whatever reason(s), the other will tend to change in response. How change occurs, both in this context and in terms of other variables in this theory, will be discussed later in the book.

GENDER DIFFERENTIATION AND SEX STRATIFICATION

Figure 2.1 shows the linkage between degree of sex stratification and degree of gender differentiation as going primarily from the former to the latter.

Scholars interested in social stratification and also minority-majority relations have often posited a series of attiudes and personality traits associated with disadvantaged status. Proponents of a "culture of poverty" (e.g., Lewis 1965; Moynihan 1965) argued that poverty, i.e, disadvantage, results in a subculture of fatalism and a short-term time perspective that prevents the deferral of gratification (see also Banfield 1958, 1968). The critics of this position usually question whether this perspective constitutes a subculture, that is, whether it is transmitted intergenerationally and comes to constitute a set of permanent personality attributes of the poor. Yet few doubt that a major response to disadvantage is the development, at least among adults, of a set of attitudes and orientations different from those of the more advantaged, superordinate strata. In addition to fatalism and a time perspective focused on the here-and-now, attributes often associated with people in social statuses below the middle class include conformity to external norms and authority, respectability, resistance to change or innovation, emphasis on the efficacy of luck rather than ability and hard work, feelings of powerlessness, and self-depreciation (Kohn 1969). The extent of disadvantage produces somewhat different attributes, which can be seen when the "lower class" is compared with the "working class," but the content of these differences is not important here. What is relevant is the fact that disadvantage produces attitudes, values, and personality traits different from those common among the advantaged.

The logical conclusion to be drawn from this tradition of research is that to the extent that one sex is more advantaged than the other in access to societal scarce and valued resources, there will tend to be differences in their attitudes, values, personalities and behaviors, whether these arise through subcultural transmission during childhood or as adult responses to their life conditions, or both.

2.5. *The greater the degree of sex stratification, the greater the degree of gender differentiation will tend to be.*

Unger (1977: 17) argued that differences in degree of power and status are better indicators of behavior than sex per se (see also Henley 1977; Meeker and Weitzel-O'Neill 1977), essentially the same argument as that made by Kanter (1976, 1977) and discussed earlier. Extensive sex stratification is in part (and perhaps most important) a question of differential power. Again, the conclusion to be drawn is that the greater the sex inequality, the greater the behavioral differences between men and women, hence the greater the perception, if not the reality, of differences in traits of personality and intellect.

The argument presented encompasses both real and perceptual levels. Inequality probably creates at least some real differences in the personality, attitudes, and values of the sexes. It also creates behavioral differences which, as argued in the last section, give rise to the perception of other kinds of differences, whether or not they exist.

Any system of inequality needs to be legitimated if it is to avoid chronic and serious challenge by the disadvantaged (Lenski 1966: 82). It is likely that this requirement for legitimation to maintain the system is especially important where the basis of inequality is ascriptive, that is, where individual differences are irrelevant compared to group characteristics in determining degree of access to societal scarce and valued resources.

2.6. *The greater the degree of sex inequality (an ascriptively based form of stratification), the greater the need for legitimation to maintain the system of inequality.*

Legitimation of sexual inequality is an issue of both gender differentiation and ideology. The latter will be specifically explored in the next section of this chapter. A high degree of gender differentiation helps to legitimate, therefore reinforce, a system of sex inequality, inasmuch as it serves to "explain" why each sex has "special competencies." In turn, there must be an ideological system that justifies differential rewards for different "special competencies" (Blau 1964). Stated in other terms:

2.7. *The greater the degree of gender differentiation, the greater the legitimacy of a system of sex inequality will tend to be.*

This proposition is represented by the connecting lines between the two social definitional variables in Figure 2.1 that link gender differentiation to sex stratification via ideology/religion. Gender stereotypes serve to buttress a given system of sex stratification by helping to legitimate it in terms of the different competencies of men and women. Recall that "different" does not mean "unequal." Therefore, in the absence of ideologies translating "different" into "unequal," gender differentiation will not directly support a system of sex inequality. It is likely, however, that where gender differentiation is very minimal, the degree of sex stratification will be low, for the society will be unable to legitimate extensive sex-based inequality. Stated otherwise, gender differentiation is a necessary but not sufficient component of legitimating a stable system of sexual inequality.

The last direct linkage of degree of gender differentiation is to the religious/ideological variable. This linkage will be discussed in the next section that focuses on the religious/ideological variable.

Degree of Ideological/Religious Support for Sex Inequality

An ideology is a coherent system of ideas that helps its adherents to understand their world, explain and evaluate events, structures and processes, and make decisions in terms of their understanding and evaluation of their world and their role in it. It thus has cognitive, evaluative, and motivational components. It may be secular or it may be sacred, in which case it is called a religion, or it may embrace both.

In the context of this theory, primary interest is focused on *dominant* ideological/religious systems within societies. By "dominant" is meant the thought system(s) to which the majority of societal members subscribe and/or the thought system(s) fostered by a powerful elite. In any case, they are institutionalized as theology, in the case of religion, and as law, in the case of a secular ideology. Not all societies are characterized by a dominant thought system, but those with no dominant ideology are postulated to be in the process of structural change, and their lack of a dominant or consensual thought system to be temporary.

Of interest here are those components of ideology/religion that pertain to sex and gender. Most societies have had and continue to have a basic religious thought system. Even in religiously diversified nations such as our own, there is a common core of Judeo-Christian theology that has traditionally had implications for the two sexes. That this core is breaking up, with different denominations taking very different positions on the roles, obligations, rights and privileges of the two sexes, is a manifestation of recent and on-going change in a variety of the variables included in this theory.

For most of human history, dominant sociopolitical ideologies have reflected religious thought. Both the masses and the elites shared beliefs rooted in religion but pertaining to the secular world, including beliefs relevant to the sexes. Minority ideologies, as well as minority religions, sometimes arose to challenge the dominant ones. The logic of this theory argues that where they succeeded in their challenge, some or many of the other variables in this theory were changing as well, if the new ideologies/theologies included new views concerning gender or sex.

In the past few decades an historically new phenomenon has arisen. In many societies, new elites have taken power and espoused ideologies not designed to be rooted in existing reality. Rather, they are oriented to producing radical socioeconomic change. Under such circumstances one may find a legally institutionalized ideology that matches neither popular consensus nor an imminent socioeconomic reality. Many such instances exist in Third World societies, and in most cases these ideologies include greater sexual equality. However, such ideologies seem to have little direct impact on degree of sex stratification until other variables enumerated in this theory also change. Stated otherwise, if such elites fail to change structural variables, ideology alone will not produce the desired changes in the relative statuses of the sexes. A case example of this phenomenon is the Soviet experience. An elite ideology of sex equality, institutionalized legally after the revolution, has so far failed to produce equality or even near-equality between men and women (Schwartz 1980). That the sexes are more equal today than at the time of the revolution can be explained by the fact that during the interim the Soviet Union changed from a predominantly agrarian to an industrialized society. The same transformation produced the same results elsewhere in the absence of a dominant ideology specifically advocating sexual equality (see Lapidus 1976; Martin and Voorhies 1975). Likewise, Kibbutz ideology of sexual equality failed to bring about the desired results in the face of structural realities covered by many variables in this theory.

The general theoretical approach underlying the discussion of this variable is essentially Marxist in origin. Societal-wide institutionalized thought systems are seen as arising out of socioeconomic structure. In turn, ideologies/religions function to reinforce that structure by legitimating it. Where a breakdown in consensus arises, it is postulated to be primarily a reflection of change in that structure. Where an elite fosters an ideology/religion not congruent with the socioeconomic reality, it will have little real impact on structure until or unless other structural variables change. In fact, the ideologies of social movements likewise typically reflect, rather than induce, the very changes sought by movement adherents. For instance, it is probable that the current feminist movement in the United States and other highly industrialized societies reflects and grew out of shifts in the economy, women's roles in the labor force, and demographic trends. In turn, movement ideology seeks to encourage and speed up the very trends which spawned it (see Chafetz 1978, chap. 6 for an analysis of the origins of the current feminist movement). In short, dominant thought systems are important forces in buttressing existing structural arrangements; alone, they are of minimal importance, except perhaps to retard change. Figure 2.2 presents the direct linkages of the variable *Degree of Ideological/Religious Support for Sex Inequality* to others in the theory.

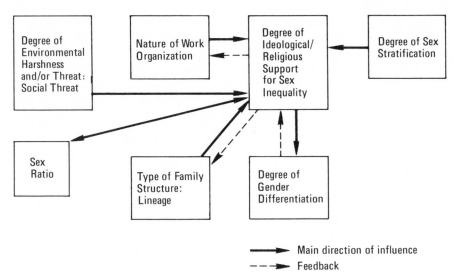

Figure 2.2   Direct Theoretical Linkages of *Degree of Ideological/Religious Support for Sex Inequality* **to Other Variables**

IDEOLOGY, GENDER DIFFERENTIATION, AND SEX STRATIFICATION

In the last section the argument was made that ideology and gender differentiation provide legitimacy to the sex stratification system; that a high degree of sex stratification is possible as a stable condition only inasmuch as extensive gender differentiation, translated by an ideology into an explanation of why "different" should entail "unequal," legitimates it. An ideology/religious thought system is broader than a set of stereotypes concerning the sexes. It places the roles, obligations, rights, and restrictions of the sexes within a total framework that justifies life in general and explains the meaning of the world, even the universe. Specific behavioral guidelines are set by a larger principle: God, "natural law," "the good of the masses," the *volk*, etc., which is accepted as the ultimate authority that can neither be questioned nor refuted. Gender stereotyping may say that women are "weak and emotional," men, "strong and rational." Judeo-Christian theology tells us that, because of Eve's transgression and attributes of irrationality, emotionality, and weakness, God has ordained that men have dominion over women. "Different" is converted into "unequal." As a broader system of ideas, ideologies/religious thought systems help give rise to specific stereotypes about the sexes; they in fact often contain some of the elements of those stereotypes within themselves.

2.8. *The greater the degree of ideological/religious support for sex inequality, the greater the degree of gender differentiation will tend to be, and vice versa.*

In turn, as indicated by the feedback arrow and the phrase "and vice versa" in the preceding proposition, popular gender stereotypes serve to reinforce ideological/religious thought systems. In the example just cited, acceptance of the injunction of male dominion over females is buttressed by a set of stereotyped beliefs concerning the relative capacities and incapacities of males and females. Certainly, dominion by one sex over the other is unjustifiable if, at a minimum, they are not generally perceived as being very different in important ways.

A caveat is in order here. It is possible that in some societies extensive gender differentiation, arising from extreme segregation of productive roles, is not associated with ideological support for inequality or a system of extensive sex stratification. Specifically, in hunting/gathering societies and horticultural, "men's work" and "women's work" are typically sharply differentiated. Yet the sexes may be defined as making more or less equally valued contributions. Under these circumstances, "different" may not be converted into "unequal." It is likely, however, that such cases are confined to sustenance societies, for reasons that will become apparent later.

Combining the insights into the more typical relationship between gender differentiation and ideology/religion with those pertaining to the relationship of legitimacy (i.e., a combination of the two definitional variables) with sexual inequality produces the following proposition:

2.9. *The greater the degree of gender differentiation, the greater the degree of ideological/religious support for sex inequality and therefore the greater the degree of sex stratification will tend to be.*

Religions that legitimize extensive sex inequality often have an ironic feature: the imputation of superior female "power" based on some supposed innate quality of the sex. This "power" is typically defined as negative and destructive, therefore requiring extensive restraint. Males are given dominion over females precisely in order to constrain their destructive potential. For instance, in Islam, the Judaism of the Old Testament, and the Christianity of the New Testament alike, female sexuality is seen as a potent force which, uncontrolled, diverts men from their duties to God. Many tribal religions impute extensive spiritual powers to women who, as supposed witches, can kill, maim, or otherwise injure others through spells. To prevent, or at least reduce, their threat, males are given a variety of "real world" powers over women. Thus, the imputation of extensive, destructive, but "other-worldly" power to women is used as a justification for an ideology stressing male superiority and dominion in this world; in turn, this ideology functions to legitimate a system of sexual inequality (see Sanday 1981, chap. 8, for a discussion of this phenomenon in technologically simple societies).

Finally, Figure 2.1 depicts a direct linkage from degree of sex strat-ification to the ideological/religious variable. This linkage reflects the logic discussed earlier; the greater the degree of sexual inequality, the more legitimating mechanisms are required to support it, if the system is to maintain itself. Thus, there will be pressure on those who profit from a system of inequality to develop and/or maintain a thought system to justify their relative advantage. Such a thought system must not only evaluate the sexes as different, but must judge their different traits individiously if differential access to societal scarce and valued resources by sex is to be legitimated.

2.10. *The greater the degree of sex stratification, the greater the degree of ideological/religious support for sex inequality will tend to be.*

The interactive effect between religious support for sexual inequality and extensive sex stratification is well exemplified in the case of agrarian societies. In general women suffer the greatest relative disadvantage in agrarian societies compared to all other societal types (Blumberg 1978: 52; Martin and Voorhies 1975: 29 ff; Nielsen 1978: 37). (The reasons for this will be discussed in later chapters.) It is important to note that most of the great world religions (e.g., Hinduism, Buddhism, Christianity, Confucianism, and Taoism) arose and/or flowered in settled agrarian societies. The other great religious systems, Judaism and Islam, arose in pastoral or mixed pastoral/agrarian societies, most of which are also characterized by relatively high degrees of sex stratification (O'Kelly 1980, chap. 5). All of these religions have in common extensive support for a system of sexual inequality (Andreas 1971: 68–77). The Hindu practices of Purdah and suttee, the Moslem practice of veiling and secluding women, the daily Orthodox Jewish prayer in which males thank God for not having made them females, St. Paul's stricture that "the husband is supreme over his wife," and the Confucian injunction to wives to distrust themselves and obey their husbands, all reflect this (see also Bird 1973; Miller and Swift 1977, chap. 5; Pagels 1976; and Ruether 1973 for further discussions of Jewish and Christian theology and sex inequality). In contrast, many "simple" societies, e.g., hunting/gathering and horticultural, practice religions consisting of a pantheon of deities, of which the chief one is often a female. Using a sample of 99 technologically simple societies, Sanday (1981: 171) reported that in societies where the sexes are equal, only one-third have origin myths involving males only, while another third have females only, and the remainder have representatives of both sexes. In contrast, among societies where males are more advantaged than females, nearly two-thirds of their origin myths involve males only, while only 12 percent involve only females.

Not only is substantial religious support for sexual inequality found in precisely those societies characterized by extensive sex stratification, but in societies where the sexes are more equal, those very same religions are transformed and/or taken less seriously. Reform Judaism, which makes many fewer invidious distinctions between the sexes than Orthodox Judaism (e.g., females are not segregated and hidden during services, they do not have to purify themselves after menstruating, and males do not repeat the prayer thanking God for not making them females), arose in Europe during the 19th century and gained widespread acceptance in Europe and North America during the 20th century, just as industrialization was decreasing the degree of sexual inequality. Moreover, while Judaism in the industrialized nations was becoming less orthodox, in the North African and Mediterranean countries, which were not industrializing, Judaism remained primarily Orthodox, even after World War II. Finally, Jews in the less economically developed central and eastern parts of Europe remained more heavily Orthodox than Western European and North American Jews until World War II. In terms of Islam, O'Kelly notes:

> where conditions support a high degree of male dominance and patriarchy, the religious practices supporting these structures are more strictly adhered to, such as among the Mediterranean herders. Where conditions do not so strongly support male supremacy, people are more likely to practice these religions indifferently, for example the Fulani and the Tuareg Moslems. [1980: 144–45]

This quotation raises the question of why, in the first place, a society characterized by a low level of sex stratification would adhere in any fashion to a religion that advocates extensive female subordination. It must be remembered that religions, specifically the universalistic religions such as Christianity and Islam, have often been spread by force of arms. Therefore, a society may have had a religion thrust upon it which had little, if any, relevance for the extant conditions of that society. The result is that the religion is not strictly adhered to, to the extent that it is incongruent with the indigenous social structure. This phenomenon probably also helps to account for the very different success rates

European colonizers have achieved in spreading Christianity to other societies.

Just as religions tend to change in response to changes in social structure, so too do secular ideologies and the legal codes that reflect them. For instance, the U.S. Constitution reflected the agrarian society in which it was created. Women were barred from political participation, reflecting an implicit ideology of extensive sexual inequality. Likewise, a number of laws at the state level, based on English Common Law as it had evolved in an agrarian context, disadvantaged women in a variety of ways (Kanowitz 1969). From the vantage point of this theory, it is not surprising that women's suffrage became a major issue after the Civil War as the Industrial Revolution gained momentum. Nor is it surprising that the second feminist movement of recent years, which during the past decade has challenged a variety of forms of female disadvantage, arose at a time when further improvements in the relative status of women were occurring due primarily to increased female labor force participation. Finally, for the same reasons, many of the laws by which women were disadvantaged changed during the 1960s and '70s, and new laws were passed directed specifically toward remedying many forms of female disadvantage (e.g., the Civil Rights Act, legislation pertaining to equal credit and equal educational opportunities). In short, structural changes (still to be analyzed) served to reduce the degree of sex stratification which, in turn, functioned to reduce the secular ideology supporting sexual inequality, as manifested in the legal code. Nor is our nation unique. Parallel changes, usually beginning with female enfranchisement, have occurred in virtually all European societies during the past century as industrialism replaced the agrarian base of society and female disadvantage decreased.

IDEOLOGY AND SEX RATIO

Comparative sex ratios constitute an all but totally ignored variable in the literature concerning gender roles and sexual inequality. A recent, groundbreaking book by the late Marcia Guttentag and Paul Secord (1983) constitutes a notable exception. Recall from Chapter 1 that the sex ratio of a given society is the total number of males compared to the total number of females, standardized on the basis of 100. Recall, also, that the range of variation around 100 is empirically much greater than is often assumed.

In Figure 2.2 the relationship between this variable and the degree of ideological/religious support for sex inequality is depicted as mutually influential. Where substantial ideological/religious support for sex inequality exists, and when the fundamental requisites needed to sustain life are in short supply (medical resources, food, water), there will be justification for, if not an injunction, that males lives be sustained first and that females receive what is left. The result will be higher deathrates for females and a high sex ratio. Moreover, if the shortage is sufficiently severe, selective female infanticide can also be readily justified. In the case of traditional India, chronic shortage even enabled the justification of adult female death through the prescribed practice of suttee, widow suicide. With no ideology supporting sex inequality, females should not die in any greater numbers than males from starvation, infanticide, or diseases associated with malnutrition. That differential evaluation of male and female lives is not uncommon, at least among simple societies, is relected by Divale's (1970) findings. His data show that among 112 different "primitive" societies, the sex ratio averaged 146, and female neglect and/or infanticide were the major causes. Guttentag and Secord (1983, chap. 3) also report findings that in medieval Europe, the less the arable land, the higher the sex ratio because of female infanticide. Moreover, the penalty for infanticide was reduced by half when the family was poor.

2.11. *The greater the degree of ideological/religious support for sex inequality, the higher the sex ratio will tend to be under conditions of fundamental scarcity of life-sustaining requisites.*

In turn, the sex ratio impacts ideology. Where a shortage of females exists, their value as workers and/or wives tends to increase. According to Guttentag and Secord (1983, chap. 1), this may be reflected in a romanticization of women, in a general lack of misogyny, and sometimes in considerable freedom for women in conducting their own lives and choosing their own mates. Guttentag and Secord support this contention with detailed analyses of views toward women among such high sex ratio groups and societies as Orthodox Jews (chap. 4) and the colonial South and frontier West of the United States (chap. 5). High sex ratios can also result in increased efforts by men to control "their" women so as not to have to share this scarce and valued "commodity." Even in the second instance, women are highly valued; the very reason for extensive male control *is* their high value, as reflected by the fact that the bride price is a common feature of high sex ratio societies (Guttentag and Secord 1983: chap. 2). But some contradictory evidence also exists on this point. It would appear that the very high sex ratio in the early days of Australian settlement produced not a high value for women, but strong male bonding and anti-female sentiments which still persist today in milder form (Desley Deacon, personal communication). Moreover, it has already been pointed out that Orthodox Judaism is characterized by extensive theological justification for sex inequality, and the same was clearly the case in the white Colonial South. Guttentag and Secord go on to argue that where an especially low sex ratio exists, women lose their value to men who are able to "pick and choose" among alternatives for mates. Under such circumstances men can often extract essentially forced labor from their wives as a condition of remaining in the relationship; misogyny flourishes, and notions of chivalry and courtliness decline.

The implication is that a society that experiences a long-term sex ratio markedly different from 100 will tend to place relatively higher value on the sex in short supply (or a lower value on the sex in oversupply) than would otherwide be the case, given all other relevant attributes of that society (see also Leibowitz 1978: 132–36). In other words, when all other variables in this theory are controlled, a skewed sex ratio will tend to reduce or mitigate an ideology of sexual inequality if it is high, or increase an ideology of inequality if it is low.

2.12. *All else being equal, the greater the departure of societal sex ratios from parity, the more likely the degree of ideological/religious support for sex inequality will be stronger if they are below 100 and weaker if they are above 100.*

IDEOLOGY AND SOCIAL THREAT

War is almost everywhere and in all times an overwhelmingly male activity (Sanday 1981: 77). Although in conditions of severe threat women have served in the military, especially in this century, rarely do they actually engage in fighting the enemy. Friedl (1975: 59–60) argues that males constitute the warriors primarily because they are biologically more expendable than females. While in an era of overpopulation, such as many societies face today, this seems to constitute a dubious explanation, for most of our species' history underpopulation was a greater problem. Excessive female deaths could therefore constitute a grave problem for societal survival in the most literal sense of failing to reproduce itself. Whether or not this constitutes the explanation for almost universally male warriors, the important phenomenon is that during wars, the most highly honored role is that of fighter, who is typically defined as "defender" of the society. Other social roles are perceived as supportive and tend to be devalued relative to the fighting role. Moreover, the more remote from the direct war effort, the more devalued supportive roles are likely to be. Thus, to the extent that males virtually monopolize the fighting roles and the bulk of the direct, militarily related support functions, their roles will tend to be more valued than those of females. In turn, the people who perform the more highly valued roles (i.e., males) are likely to be more highly valued (Friedl 1975: 20). As Brownmiller argued:

> War provides men with the perfect psychologic backdrop to give vent to their contempt for women. The very maleness of the military—the brute power of weaponry exclusive to their hands, the spiritual bonding of men at arms, the manly discipline of orders given and orders obeyed . . . confirms for men what they long suspect, *that women are peripheral, irrelevant to the world that counts,* passive spectators to the action in the center ring. [1975: 25–26, emphasis added]

The relationship between social threat and ideology is depicted in Figure 2.2 as flowing from the former to the latter and can be expressed as the following proposition:

2.13. *The more a society engages in warfare, the greater its ideological/ religious support for sex inequality will tend to be.*

The great empire-building societies (e.g., classical Rome, Great Britain in the 19th century, and China) have often been characterized by secular and religious systems that devalue women. Nazi Germany provides a particularly clear example of this phenomenon. Its ideology of "kitchen, children and church" for women stressed the familial and subordinate role of females, essentially barring them from positions of power and influence (Rupp 1977). This reversed a gradual decrease in emphasis on sexual inequality resulting from the late 19th- and early 20th-century industrialization of Germany. Islam, spread by force of arms, glorified the warrior and devalued women, as did feudal Japan and the Japanese empire of this century. As military conflict on the American Great Plains intensified, Sanday (1981: 147, 157) notes, the status of Cheyenne and Comanche women decreased. In fact, among 119 technologically simple societies, Sanday (1981: 174) finds that in 82 percent of those where males are advantaged over females, warfare is chronic, compared to only 50 percent of those societies where the sexes are equal. Moreover, in those societies where the sexes are essentially equal but a myth of male dominance exists, 78 percent are involved in chronic warfare. Men need to be motivated to risk their lives in warfare. Such motivation can be found, in part, in an ideology that defines them as superior to women inasmuch as they are warlike and brave, and prepared to die for their god, their nation, their class, or their ideals.

It should be noted, however, that where chronic warfare removes males from their home communities for extended periods of time (as much as several years), females may actually receive some advantages that would not otherwise accrue to them. Since they must often assume the productive roles normally engaged in by males, and also because they are not under the daily scrutiny and control of male kin, women may actually benefit substantially from warfare—at least in the short run until the men return (see, for instance, Sanday's discussion of the Abipon and the Seneca, 1981: 121 and 117; see also Whyte, 1978b: 129). This point is vividly illustrated in the recent movie "Rosie the Riveter" in its depiction of American women in factory work during World War II.

IDEOLOGY, WORK, AND FAMILY STRUCTURE

In the outset of this section the point was made that in this theory, ideology is considered primarily as a reflection of existing structural phenomena which, in turn, are reinforced by ideological phenomena. Perhaps the single most-important aspect of structure in explaining a dominant sex-related ideology is the nature of work organization. It will be recalled that this variable is a composite of several important variables, including the division of productive labor by sex, control over the means of production, and control over the products of production. The relationship posited by this theory between work and ideology, depicted in Figure 2.2, can be stated propositionally:

2.14. *The more females contribute to the productive efforts of their society and the more they control the means and products of production, the less the degree of ideological/religious support for sex inequality will tend to be.*

Societies that produce for sustenance only are typically hunting/ gathering or simple horticultural in their economic bases. In these types of societies females typically produce a substantial part, if not the majority, of the total food supply. For instance, in hunting/gathering societies, women furnish up to 80 percent of the food by gathering fruits, nuts, grains, roots, and hunting small game (Blumberg 1978: 6–7; Boulding 1976: 96; Martin and Voorhies 1975, chap. 7). Most gardening work in simple horticultural societies, except for clearing new fields, is also done by women, who probably originally developed cultivation from knowledge gained as gatherers (Boulding 1976: 97; Nielsen 1978: 26).

Under such conditions, women would also tend to control their very simple means of production—a digging stick, simple containers, a hoe—and be able to dispense with the products of production as freely as men are able to dispense with their products (mostly larger game). As Lenski (1966: 46) points out, in sustenance-based societies the general principle of distribution, applicable to women and men, is based on altruism;

food gets shared so that all may survive, regardless of an individual's success in obtaining food on any given day. Thus, hunting/gathering societies are characterized by very minimal sex stratification (Boulding 1976: 96; Leibowtiz 1978; Martin and Voorhies 1975: 189; Nielsen 1978: 22, 25–26; Van den Berghe 1973: 73; Whyte 1978: 129), as are simple horticultural societies. Under such circumstances, it would be unlikely that an ideology supporting substantial sexual inequality would emerge. Females produce and control a major share of the life-sustaining requisites, and males would have little basis upon which to argue for superiority. In fact, attempts to do so might be met with an abrogation of the altruism principle by females. Some minimal ideology of male superiority may exist, inasmuch as in both societal types men provide the bulk of animal protein. With a simple technology, the hunt for large game is often not very successful. In turn, scarcity of animal protein tends to make it the most highly prized food (Friedl 1975: 13; Sanday 1981: 124). Yet a full-blown ideology of sexual inequality requires more important differences in the relative contributions of each sex to the collective well-being.

In surplus-producing societies, the means of production are typically more elaborate, expensive, and/or scarce than in sustenance societies, which are based on a simpler technology. Because of this, not everyone may have access to ownership of his/her own means of production, and ownership or control may be divorced from use. The owners will often be those who, for whatever reasons, are able to amass more wealth than others. They are then often able to cajole or coerce others into doing the actual labor, and returning much or all of the surplus to the owners as payment for use of the means of production. Thus the division of actual labor may no longer predict control over the means and products or production. In such societies, maintenance of the system will require an ideology that justifies the superiority of those who control surplus production, regardless of who produces that surplus. Such an ideology will probably proclaim that those who own the means of production make a greater contribution to the collective well-being than those who "merely" provide the labor.

For a variety of reasons to be discussed in detail in the next two chapters, surplus-producing societies, whether advanced horticultural, agrarian, or industrial in economic base, tend to be characterized by two phenomena: (a) greater relative contributions by males to economic productivity than is characteristic of their sex in sustenance-based societies, and, more important, (b) greater control over the means and products of production by males, primarily through the development of patrilineality, than is characteristic of sustenance societies (see Engels 1968: 495; Martin and Voorhies 1975: 223 ff.; Schlegel 1972: 80). Stated otherwise, just as Lenski (1966: 46) and, long before him, Engels (1968) argued that social or class inequality depends upon, and arises concomitant with, the development of an economic surplus, so too does a substantial degree of sexual inequality arise concomitant with surplus production (see also Whyte 1978b). In turn, it can be supposed that with increased control over the means and products of production by males, an ideology/religion supportive of sexual inequality will tend to develop to legitimate that control, just as ideologies/religions develop to legitimate social class inequality.

In the preceding paragraph it was asserted that in surplus-producing societies males gain greater control over the means and products of production primarily through the development of patrilineage. The lineage structure of a society can take many forms. In this theory, two extremes are defined and all other forms are viewed as intermediate. The extremes are, of course, matrilineage and patrilineage. The latter cannot occur unless the society understands enough about reproductive biology to perceive the male role in "producing" offspring. Even where that is understood, however, as will become clear in Chapters 3 and 4, patrilineage does not tend to occur in the absence of other identifiable economic and environmental phenomena.

Matrilineality tends to be associated with a relatively low degree of sex stratification, patrilineality often (but not always) with substantial female disadvantage (Martin and Voorhies 1975: 225). In a system of patrilineage, not only is descent reckoned through the male line, but there is a tendency for inheritance to flow disproportionately, even totally in some societies, through males (see Gouldner and Peterson's study of 71 preindustrial societies, 1962: 21). The converse is not necessarily true of matrilineal societies, many of which have an avuncular component that includes inheritance for males through their maternal uncle. Moreover, matrilineage is overwhelmingly confined to non-surplus societies—those with few goods that are inheritable. Patrilineage, on the other hand, is found most often in surplus-producing societies where considerable inheritable wealth may be generated. In other words, matrilineage requires little ideological/religious legitimation to maintain itself, because its ramifications do not typically entail male disadvantage. Patrilineage, however, requires substantial legitimation to maintain itself in light of its typically disadvantageous ramifications for females.

2.15. *Patrilineal societies will tend to have a higher degree of ideological/ religious support for sex inequality than those characterized by other lineage forms, and vice versa.*

Figure 2.2 depicts this relationship plus a feedback mechanism, manifested also by the phrase "and vice versa" in Proposition 2.15. Where substantial ideological support for sex inequality exists, this will increase the tendency to define one's heritage through higher-status male kin and to reserve wealth for higher-status male offspring.

Conclusions

In this chapter two social definitional variables—*Degree of Gender Differentiation* and *Degree of Ideological/Religious Support for Sex Inequality*—have been examined in terms of their relationship to one another and to the other variables to which they have a direct linkage in this theory. The general conclusion to be drawn is that together they normally function (that is, during periods of relative stasis) to legitimate existing structural arrangements, from which they arise; assessments of gender differences are converted into judgments of differential value, which legitimate differential rewards to the sexes. Change in structure tends to produce social definitional changes supportive of the newly emerging structural reality. The remainder of this book will examine these structural phenomena, beginning in the next chapter with the single most important set of variables, collectively termed the *Nature of Work Organization.*

3

THE WORK ORGANIZATION VARIABLES

Several aspects of the way in which a society organizes productive labor comprise the compound variable *Nature of Work Organization*. In Chapter 1 six dimensions were mentioned: (a) the division of tasks in terms of the relative contributions of each sex to surplus and sustenance production, with the former typically being more highly valued socially; (b) the extent to which one sex monopolizes ownership or control over the means of production; (c) the extent to which one sex monopolizes ownership or control over the products of production; (d) the relative replaceability of the labor done by members of one sex, either by a reserve labor force of their own sex or by members of the other sex; (e) the extent to which the productive roles in a society are sex-segregated; and (f) the extent to which productive roles require lengthy attention spans for their accomplishment.

In the last section of Chapter 2, a clear conceptual distinction between inequality and ownership/control of the means and products of production was not made. If the two cannot be conceptually differentiated, then it is tautological to say that the latter affects the former. Recall that one of the indicators of degree of sex stratification mentioned in Chapter 1 refers to the extent to which the sexes have equal access to the material goods available in a society. Ownership or control of the means and products of production is a form of wealth. It is clear that those who possess such wealth, by definition, have greater access to at least some kinds of material goods than others in their society. In this sense, these dimensions of the work organization variable overlap the stratification variable. Non-owners can be very unequal in their access to material goods, however. Moreover, in industrial societies at least, there are owners whose share of ownership is so small that their access to material goods is equal to, or less than that of many salaried non-owners. In these cases, the two variables do not overlap. Wealth in the form of ownership or control over the means and products of production may be viewed as one among several possible means (albeit a very important one) for attaining access to scarce societal resources, material and otherwise. The comparative *extent* of such access, not the reasons for it, is part of the definition of the dependent variable *Degree of Sex Stratification*. For these reasons, ownership or control of the means and products of production is considered to be conceptually distinct from the degree of sex stratification, although the two are linked empirically.

The linkages between components of work organization, on the one hand, and the two social definitional variables, on the other, were explored in the last chapter and will not be repeated here. The linkages between work organization and all other variables that are directly linked to this set in the theory are depicted in Figure 3.1.

Work Organization and Sex Stratification

The linkage between work organization and degree of sex stratification postulates the direction of influence as going primarily from the former to the latter. Some aspects of this linkage have already been mentioned. In the discussion immediately above, ownership/control over the means and/or products of production was conceptually distinguished from sex stratification, but it was clear that the two are empirically related.

3.1. *The more males disproportionately own/control the means and/or products of production, the greater the degree of sex stratification will tend to be.*

The logic behind this proposition is simple. To the extent that males disproportionately control the means of production, they will be able to appropriate—that is, control—the products of production, regardless of who actually does the work of producing. To the extent that they control the products of production, it can be assumed that any surplus over and above that required to sustain life will tend to flow disproportionately to themselves. In other words, control over the products of production allows the controller to convert those products into a variety of forms of scarce and valued societal resources—be they material, services, formal or informal power, leisure, etc.—through some mechanism of exchange. Therefore, just as a social class which disproportionately controls the means and products of production is able to, and typically does, enjoy greater access to a wide range of societal scarce and valued resources, so too will males enjoy substantial advantage over females

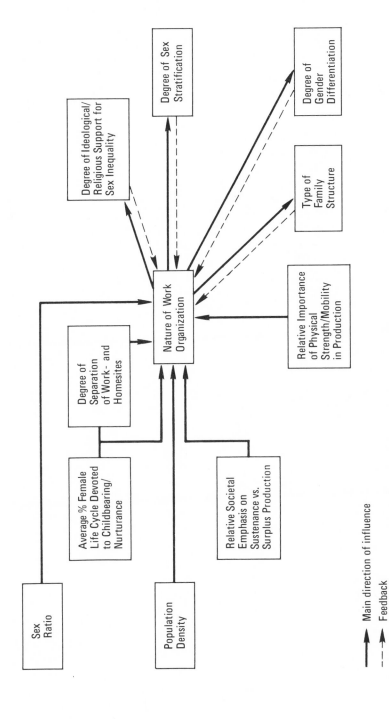

Main direction of influence
Feedback

Figure 3.1 Direct Theoretical Linkages of *Nature of Work Organization* **to Other Variables**

where they disproportionately control the means and products of production.

Indeed, as a general principle it can be asserted that those who control the products of production can (and often do) use them to involve themselves in a network of exchange (see Friedl 1975). In turn, this results in the ability to call upon the support of others whose obligations have been incurred through prior acceptance of goods. Such support constitutes the basis of superior power and status. For this reason, involvement in the extradomestic sphere is necessary, but not sufficient, for high status, inasmuch as only such involvement can create reciprocity obligations outside the family. It is interesting to note Friedl's explanation that the slight male advantage in hunting/gathering societies is based upon the fact that animal protein, which is controlled by men, is exchanged extradomestically, while vegetable products, which are controlled by women, are normally distributed only within the family (1975: 21–22).

Where females disproportionately control the means and products of production, they will not be *more* advantaged than males, for reasons discussed in Chapter 1. Nonetheless, there is apt to be a low level of sex stratification, i.e., substantial sexual equality. Likewise, female disadvantage will not be great where the sexes more equally share in the ownership/control of the means and products of production (see Friedl 1975).

The extent of sex differences in control of the means and products of production is integrally bound up with lineage patterns and will be explored more fully later. Sex differences in ownership/control are also partially related to the sexual division of labor (see Bourguignon 1980: 6). Where males approach a monopoly of productive roles, they are likely to disproportionately control the means and products of production. For instance, in our society, where until recently females constituted only a small minority of labor force participants, they have historically constituted about 40 percent of the top wealthholders and about half of the individual stockholders (U.S. Bureau of Census 1976: 425). Yet de facto control typically has resided in the hands of male relatives, attorneys, or bankers (Amundsen 1971: 52, 93–95; see also Tickamyer 1981). Moreover, in most states in the United States persons who earned an income legally controlled that income. Since, until recently, relatively few women were wage earners, that meant that their access to money was almost entirely dependent upon the generosity of their male supporters. While husbands were legally responsible for the economic maintenance of their families, there was no mechanism to ensure such support except in the instance of divorce, and even then the de facto extent of support was (and remains) typically minimal, on the average.

It is safe to assert, therefore, that until the recent, dramatic increase in female labor force participation, American males had a near monopoly of control over the means and products of production. In socialist/communist societies, control over the means and products of production is exercised by political leaders and high-level managers, positions overwhelmingly filled by men. In short, regardless of type of political economy, relatively extensive sex stratification exists where males play the primary productive role.

Where females constitute the primary producers, they may indeed disproportionately own/control the means and products of production, such as in some horticultural societies, which are also characterized by low levels of sex stratification. For instance, Martin and Voorhies cite Brown's (1970) research and conclusions concerning the Iroquois (see also Sanday's discussion of the Iroquois, 1981: 24–28):

> the key to elevated status for Iroquois women lay in their relationship to production and distribution of wealth. As in a great number of horticultural societies, women were the exclusive cultivators. However, a frequent accompaniment to matriliny—the manipulation of access rights to seeds and to arable land by matrilineal descent groups themselves—gave Iroquois women exclusive control over the production and storage of food. *They were not only the primary producers, but collectively owned the means of production as well.* [Martin and Voorhies 1975: 226, emphasis added]

In other horticultural societies females are the primary producers, but they work as virtual slaves for the benefit of male kin. In discussing patrilineal horticultural societies, Martin and Voorhies argue:

> women continue their role as primary cultivators but . . . the relationship of women to land and resources is now a consequence of marriage rather than descent. . . . they become economic producers for and domestic *appendages* of their . . . *male spouses.* Control of land and resource allocation is thus transferred to the manipulators and caretakers of the new economy. [1975: 235–36, emphasis added]

The difference is probably accounted for largely by other variables that impact family structure, to be discussed later.

It has been noted several times that surplus or exchange production is everywhere more highly valued than sustenance production. Therefore:

3.2. *In surplus-producing societies, the greater the contribution of females to the production of surplus goods, the less the sex stratification tends to be.*

Where males monopolize surplus production, no matter how fundamental the contributions of females to sustenance, the latter will tend to be disadvantaged. Moreover, if the females' contributions to sustenance are small, they will be even more disadvantaged.

3.3. *Except where females contribute to producing a surplus, the less their contributions to producing sustenance goods, the greater the sex stratification tends to be.*

In short, combining propositions 3.2 and 3.3, where females are largely absent from the productive activities of their society, they will be most highly disadvantaged. Where they participate heavily in the most highly valued productive activities, they will tend to approach equality (see Etienne and Leacock 1980: 14). Finally, where they are productively active, but not in the highly valued sphere of surplus production, their relative status is intermediary. Combining propositions 3.2 and 3.3 produces a more general one:

3.4. *The greater the involvement of females in the most important (highly valued) productive roles in their societies, the less the degree of sex stratification will tend to be, and vice versa.*

Examples of the first instance are most agrarian and many pastoral societies, where females contribute little to production and are largely confined to the reproductive/private sphere. Female disadvantage, as noted earlier, tends to be greatest in these types of society (Martin and Voorhies 1975, chaps. 9 and 10; O'Kelly 1980, chaps. 5 and 6). Thus, for instance, using a sample of 93 agrarian societies, Martin and Voorhies found that in 81 percent, males monopolize cultivation activities (1975: 283). As O'Kelly concludes from her examination of agrarian societies, "the subordination of women reaches its highest degree in these societies" (1980: 190).

The intermediate situation is exemplified in many surplus-producing horticultural societies, where women produce much, if not most, of the sustenance goods. Of 104 horticultural societies in Martin and Voorhies's sample, only 17 percent assigned cultivation exclusively to males, while half assigned it exclusively to females (1975: 283). In turn, they note that even in patrilineal horticultural societies, women are able to maintain substantial independence, unlike the situation in agrarian societies.

An example of the other extreme was the first generation of Kibbutz settlers. Women participated equally with men in the fields in a context where agricultural work was the most highly valued form of labor. There was virtually no sex stratification (O'Kelly 1980: 309). For reasons to be discussed later, within a generation few women remained in agricultural tasks, and female status and power, relative to male, decreased; that is, sex stratification increased (see Blumberg 1978: 112–16). Conversely, in the West, as societies evolved from agrarian, with relatively little female contribution to surplus production, to the more advanced stages of industrial, with substantial female involvement in surplus production, the relative status of women increased, as noted earlier.

Proposition 3.4 implies feedback with the phrase "and vice versa." It is likely that where females are relatively highly disadvantaged because of their minimal contributions to important productive activities, barriers might be erected by the powerful (males) to prevent or make it difficult for women to engage in highly valued work, thus protecting male access to valued jobs. This statement is exemplified by the myriad of state-level "protective" laws, which, until recently, denied many American women access to such jobs as bartender, to many crafts, and to assembly-line jobs entailing lifting moderate weights, night-time work, etc. Union restrictions may, and in the past frequently have, also served the same function (Berch 1982, chap. 3), as have job preference for veterans after a war. The power of the dominant group, the males, is used to restrict for themselves access to socially valued work which, in turn, reinforces their collective advantages.

The fourth dimension of work organization refers to the relative replaceability of women's labor (see Blumberg 1978: 26–27).

3.5. *The more replaceable women workers are, the greater the degree of sex stratification will tend to be.*

Recall that women can be replaceable because the work they do is of such a nature that other nonemployed females or males can readily substitute for them. Women are replaceable by women only if there is a surplus of women. This occurs either because of high female unemployment or underemployment, or because males are able to capture women by raiding other societies. The latter is characteristic of many simple societies, the former of many industrial societies.

Women are not replaceable by men if they perform tasks requiring skills possessed only or mostly by women (see Blumberg 1979: 124). For instance, few males in the United States today can replace females as nurses, grammar school teachers, or secretaries (although there are many women in the "reserve" labor force who could do so). This issue leads directly to the fifth dimension of work organization mentioned at the outset of this chapter: degree of occupational segregation.

3.6. The greater the occupational segregation by sex, the less males will tend to be able to replace females. Therefore:

3.7. In the absence of a surplus of potential female workers, the greater the occupational segregation by sex, the less the degree of sex stratification will tend to be.

At first glance proposition 3.7 seems to contradict the assertion made in Chapter 1 that sex-segregated occupations have been found to be linked with female disadvantage. However, this *empirical* relationship is characteristic of Western industrialized societies, virtually all of which have a large pool of adult females who are not in the labor force, a "reserve labor force." A very large number of women trained as nurses, teachers, and typists are full-time homemakers who, under the right inducements (e.g., war, inflation), can and have been pulled into the labor market. Where such a reserve exists, proposition 3.5 better explains the empirical relationship between occupational sex segregation and female disadvantage.

In summary, sex segregation by occupation protects women from competition by men, enhancing their relative position. But it enhances their relative position only if there is no surplus of women skilled in the female-segregated occupations (Blumberg 1979: 124), which is typically not the case in industrial societies, although it may be in some horticultural and hunting/gathering ones. Women in the U.S. labor force, for instance, are overwhelmingly located in a handful of occupations. In 1970, half of all employed women were found in 17 occupations, while 63 occupations accounted for half the employed males (Kanter 1977: 16). Moreover, the occupations in which the vast majority of women are employed are each comprised of 80 percent or more female workers (Berch 1982: 71). Because the number of "appropriate" female occupations has been so small, far more women have been trained for them at *some* time in their lives than can usually be absorbed in the labor force at any *given time*. A shortage of nurses, for instance, does not mean that there are too few women trained as nurses; it means that there are not enough trained women willing to do such work at a particular time, given existing salaries, work conditions, etc. In short, a major characteristic of heavily female-dominated occupations in the industrialized world is that most of the time there exists a reserve labor force of replacements who are not in the active labor force but possess the requisite skills. Being readily replaceable reduces women's value to employers, resulting in fewer rewards than their skill-level might otherwise indicate.

For males, sex segregation tends to work almost entirely to their advantage. Not only is it difficult to replace them with women, given that almost all adult males are engaged in productive labor in most societies, there is no large "reserve" of their own sex available. This may not be the case in simple horticultural societies, but it has already been noted that in such societies males tend not to be very advantaged relative to women, which may now be partially attributable to their "replaceability" as workers. In industrial societies, periods of high unemployment (recessions, depressions) may produce a surplus of male workers. But since they also produce an increased surplus of females, the statuses of the sexes relative to one another are not affected. Indeed, economic downturns appear to produce greater increases in female than male unemployment rates (Berch 1982: 17–18).

Family Structure and Work Organization

In Figure 3.1, the linkage between work organization and family structure depicts the main direction of influence as flowing from the former to the latter, with a feedback mechanism. As Saffioti argued concerning Brazil (as paraphrased by Leacock 1978: x): "Women's position [in the economy] then, is not so much based on family demands . . . as family structure itself is based on the [economic] marginalization of women" (see also Friedl 1975: 8, 60). One exception to the postulated direction of influence was mentioned earlier. It was suggested, and will be discussed further, that lineage patterns affect which, if either, sex disproportionately owns/controls the means and products of production. As will become apparent, however, lineage patterns themselves are affected by work organization variables. In this section three components of family structure will be examined as they relate to aspects of the organization of productive work: lineage, locality, and the division of household, or reproductive/private sphere, labor.

LINEAGE, LOCALITY, AND WORK ORGANIZATION

Lineage and locality structures tend to vary together. Matrilineage is often associated with matrilocality (or at least avunculocality). Patrilineage is less often associated with patrilocality, but the latter is not typically found in the absence of the former (Gouldner and Peterson 1962: 21). Bilateral descent and neolocality are also associated, although the latter may also be found with patrilineage.

Almost all known matrilineal/matrilocal societies have been simple, non-surplus-producing, horticultural societies (Blumberg 1978: 42; Friedl 1975: 50; Schlegel 1972: 17). In a sample of 104 horticultural societies, Martin and Voorhies (1975: 219) found that nearly a quarter were matrilineal, a quarter were matrilocal or avunculocal, and nearly 17 percent were both. They argue that the matrilineal/matrilocal horticultural societies tend to be more technologically simple and sustenance-oriented than the patrilineal/patrilocal horticultural societies. Matrilineal/matrilocal societies also tend to be found in environments which are not harsh physically or socially.

Martin and Voorhies's explanation of lineage/locality types basically is as follows (see also Sanday 1981: 116): co-workers who are related by blood and life-long acquaintance do their productive work together with less friction and more efficiency than other co-workers. Where the chief function of a society is sustenance, and where that sustenance is provided mostly by women (i.e., simple, non-surplus-producing horticultural societies), then smooth and efficient female work groups are provided by matrilineage and matrilocality. This places together unrelated men who meet after marriage, and maintains women with female kin of life-long acquaintance. An emphasis on surplus production and/or production in difficult environments places a much higher premium on male contributions to productive labor. Employing the same logic, males related by blood and life-long acquaintance work more efficiently, with less hostility and more cooperation, than other men. Hence, patrilineage and patrilocality arise, often after transition through avunculocality or other intermediate forms, as a function of greater male involvement in productive activities, as simple horticultural societies evolve into surplus-producing, advanced horticultural societies. They also exist in non-surplus-producing, simple horticultural societies which live in an environment difficult to cultivate. (As an aside, to be examined in the next chapter, chronic warfare also places a premium on male cooperation, thus spurring patrilineality and patrilocality.)

3.8. *The more the productive enterprises of a society enhance the importance of cohesive work groups comprised of one sex, the more likely the lineage patterns will flow through that sex and the locality patterns will maintain physical proximity of related members of that sex.*

This argument is predicated on the fact that the contribution of one sex to the productivity of the society is considerably greater than that of the other sex. In simple horticultural societies women do most of the regular productive work. Men's work consists of periodic hunting, the provision of political and religious leadership, and such occasional and relatively arduous horticultural tasks as clearing the land for new gardens to replace plots depleted by cultivation (Boulding 1976: 97).

In hunting/gathering societies, both sexes work separately in sex-segregated groups, each of which makes important and regular contributions to their society. The result is that there is no strong emphasis on lineality and no consistent pattern of locality (Leibowitz 1978: 15; Martin and Voorhies 1975: 186). For example, of 90 such societies in a sample examined by Martin and Voorhies (1975: 185), 60 were neither patrilineal nor matrilineal.

In pastoral societies, where females typically produce little, patrilineality is nearly universal (Martin and Voorhies 1975: 344). Likewise, in agrarian societies, where the bulk of the productive labor is also provided by males, patrilineage and patrilocality are common. In their sample of such societies, Martin and Voorhies (1975: 287) found that 66 percent were patrilocal and 50 percent patrilineal. They also found that this represents a change from the more advanced horticultural societies in the direction of more bilateral and neolocal structures, and somewhat fewer that were patrilineal and patrilocal. They argue that this decrease in male-dominated lineage and locality is the result of more individualized landholdings, which result in work patterns no longer heavily based on large, cohesive work groups. Moreover, bilateral, neolocal families are better adapted to the more urban, market-oriented societies characteristic of agrarian-based economies relative to the horticultural. Such families are more mobile and therefore able to follow economic opportunities.

Finally, bilateral and neolocal families are the norm in industrial societies, where the trends toward urban living, market-based economies, and extensive geographical mobility reach their height. In short, lineage/locality structures reflect more than sex segregation and monopoly of productive labor, but these variables do influence family structure, at least in technologically simple societies.

Given that matrilineality and patrilineality reflect, in part, the contributions of the sexes to the productive enterprises of their respective societies, it is likely, as mentioned earlier, that they affect the extent to which one sex monopolizes ownership/control over the means and products of production. Where women are the primary producers and enhance their work efforts through matrilineality and matrilocality, it is reasonable to assume that they disproportionately control the means (hence products) of production, which are transmitted intergenerationally through their own lineage to daughters who will provide the bulk of the next generation of labor (Aberle 1973: 655–730; Gouldner and Peterson 1962: 21). Such control, as mentioned earlier, results in a low level of sex stratification, i.e., minimal female disadvantage, a characteristic of matrilineal and matrilocal societies (Blumberg 1978: 43–44; Martin and Voorhies 1975: 224–25; Schlegel 1972: 98, 101–2; Whyte 1978b: 132–33). Likewise, patrilineage and patrilocality tend to result in disproportionate male control over the means and products of production, resulting in extensive sex stratification or female disadvantage

(Gouldner and Peterson 1962: 21; Nielsen 1978: 30). This is sometimes mitigated by extensive female contribution to production in such societies (e.g., advanced horticultural ones), just as males are not actually disadvantaged (only less advantaged) in matrilineal/matrilocal societies because of their contributions to production/public sphere activities.

3.9. *Where the lineage and locality structures reflect a one-sex basis, that sex will tend to disproportionately own/control the means and products of production.*

WORK ORGANIZATION AND THE DIVISION OF HOUSEHOLD LABOR

In Chapter 1 it was stated that females are nowhere superior to males in overall status because they are never able to specialize totally in the productive/public sphere of life. Males are able to, however, and do so in many societies, and where they do their relative advantage over females tends to be extensive. The extent to which males share the tasks associated with the reproductive/private sphere of life is postulated as being associated with the extent to which females are engaged in the productive/public sphere of life.

3.10. *The more males monopolize the productive/public sphere roles, the more females monopolize the reproductive/private sphere roles, and vice versa.*

Stated otherwise, the division of labor within the family reflects the extent to which females play an important role in economic production. Where females contribute little to production, especially surplus production, as in many agrarian and pastoral societies, they tend to be solely responsible for the reproductive/private sphere tasks. Male involvement in that sphere should be greatest where females contribute extensively to the important economic activities of their society. For instance, Friedl (1975: 61) notes that in horticultural societies men do their own domestic work, inasmuch as they live apart in their own communal houses. Of course, once household labor comes to be defined as an exclusively female preserve, the ability of women to participate in economic activity is curtailed, as their time and energy are consumed in the reproductive/private sphere. In other words, feedback occurs between the household division of labor and the division of productive labor, as indicated in Proposition 3.10 by the phrase "and vice versa."

In hunting/gathering and horticultural societies, where women tend to make major contributions to productive labor, it appears that males are often heavily involved in child-care and in whatever simple domestic tasks are required (see, for instance, Leibowitz's discussion of the Andaman Islanders, 1978: 173–76). Murray and Alvarez (1975) also find extensive male involvement among Haitians, whose women constitute the economic mainstay through their trading activities. Conversely, among the Hausa, "women do not contribute much to food production, and men are only distantly involved with their children" (Sanday 1981: 35).

While only tangentially related to this argument, Sanday's findings (1981: 61) concerning paternal involvement with their offspring and sex emphasis of origin myths, in a sample of 95 technologically simple societies, are interesting. Where the origin myth centers on females only, 63 percent of societies are characterized by regular or frequent close contact between fathers and children, compared to 17 percent of societies whose myths center on males. Conversely, only 6 percent of the former, but 34 percent of the latter societies are characterized by rare to no instances of close contact between fathers and their children. If it can be assumed that in societies which center their origin myths around females, their status and contributions to productive work tend to be high and, conversely, where the myth emphasizes males only, female status and possibly productive contributions are lower, then these findings offer strong support for hypothesis 3.10. Sanday's discussion of a number of case studies makes these assumptions tenable.

Of course, myriad examples can be found in contemporary industrial societies of females who constitute a significant proportion of the labor force while males contribute little to household labor. Males in the Soviet Union are one example of this phenomenon (Schwartz 1979; Berch 1982: 189), as are U.S. males married to full-time employed wives. Such men contribute an average of less than 5 hours a week to household labor, and their wives more than 30 (Barrett 1976; Kahne 1976). In computing the total contributions of each sex to reproductive/private sphere tasks, however, attention should also be paid to unmarried adults. In contemporary postindustrial societies, many males live unattached to females, either as bachelors or as divorcés. These males often contribute a substantial amount of time and effort to household tasks, i.e., their own maintenance and sometimes part-time maintenance of children. Adding this to the contributions of married males, it is likely that, relative to the sharp segregation of public/private sphere roles characteristic of agrarian societies, and the early stages of industrialization when females constitute a smaller proportion of the labor force than they do in postindustrial societies, male contribution to the private sphere is greater in postindustrial society. In the early stages of industrialization, as well as in agrarian societies, divorce is less frequent, and unmarried males tend to live at home under the domestic care of their mothers and sisters. The approach suggested here implies that postin-

dustrial societies may be experiencing culture lag in terms of married
couples' division of household labor. If that is the case, if high levels
of married female labor force participation continue, married male, hence
total male, contributions to reproductive/private sphere labor should
increase with time. This implies the logical extension of Proposition
3.10.

3.11. *The greater the contributions made by females to the productive/
public sphere activities, the greater the contributions made by males to the
reproductive/private sphere activities will tend to be, and vice versa.*

Again, feedback is indicated in this proposition. Where males share
household tasks, females are freed to assume a greater share of productive
tasks. As they do so, the extent of female disadvantage tends to decrease.

Surplus Production and Work Organization

Only three societal types are based entirely on sustenance activity:
hunting/gathering, simple horticultural, and many, but not all, pastoral.
Except for the sustenance-based pastoral societies, non-surplus societies
are generally characterized by the fact that women contribute substantially
to the productive enterprise, often gathering or growing most of the
food supply. In return, as already noted, these societies, unlike pastoral
and the surplus-producing ones, are characterized by low levels of sex
stratification. In contrast, in most surplus-producing societies, males are
heavily involved in the basic productive enterprises of their society,
especially in the production of surplus goods. In many (e.g., agrarian)
they virtually monopolize production.

Historically, surplus production first developed in horticultural societies. Sahlins (1972, chap. 3) argues that in horticultural societies, the
development of political authority which overarches individual domestic
units contributes to an increased emphasis on surplus production. The
chief, or "big man," and other leaders use their authority to encourage
the development of a surplus to be used for their further status ag-
grandizement. Political authority appears to be nearly universally a male-
dominated activity; the existence of ancient matriarchy has yet to be
demonstrated empirically and thus remains in the status of the mythical
(Van den Berghe 1973: 53). The theoretical question here is a classic
chicken-and-egg issue: which comes first, surplus production that involves
males to a greater extent, thus creating male-dominated lineage and
political structures, or male-dominated political and kin structures that
encourage surplus production? From the point of view of the theory
presented here, Sahlins's argument offers no mechanism to explain the

evolution from non-surplus, matrilineal, matrilocal, horticultural societies to patrilineal, surplus-producing, politically more complex societies. To the extent that males do not control, and indeed are relatively secondary to the productive activities of their society, upon what basis would they be able to develop kinship dominance and extensive political authority? In other words, the theory presented here reverses Sahlins's argument. While agreeing that surplus production is related to more complex and male-dominated family and political structures, it is postulated that *such structures arise primarily as a result of greater male participation in production activities*, which in turn arises from efforts to produce a surplus. Once the new structures are in existence, however, it is altogether likely that they further spur surplus production. In turn, it is likely that, as suggested in Chapter 1, the impetus to produce a surplus comes from threat or insecurity. The threat may be periodic food shortage and/or hostile human communities, but the result is an attempt to bind non-kin together through exchange networks, which depend on surplus to exchange.

3.12. *Change from a sustenance-based to a surplus-producing economy tends to result in an increase in male participation in productive labor, focussed on the production of surplus goods.*

Given that this increased male involvement in production tends to alter family structure away from the matrilineal/matrilocal and toward the patrilineal/patrilocal, and given proposition 3.9, then:

3.13. *The development of a surplus-oriented economy will tend to decrease the extent to which females own/control the means and products of production and increase the extent to which males do.*

Before I continue with an explication of the theory, a brief digression is in order. At least since Engels (1968) wrote his famous essay "The Origin of the Family, Private Property and the State" in 1884, communists, socialists, and today many radical feminists, as well, have argued that the root of sex inequality is to be found in private property, and the development of class stratification. As a logical corollary to this assertion, the abolition of private property, i.e., the abolition of the institution of class inequality, should eventuate in sex equality as well. The logic of the argument developed in this book does not totally contradict this position. Rather, it views sex inequality as more complex in origin. It is posited that a major factor in the initial development of sex inequality is indeed the development of economic surplus, which is closely related to the development of class systems. Nevertheless, this model postulates a number of other important factors related to the development of sex inequality, independent of this one. The logic of this approach is that the abolition of private property is certainly not *sufficient* to result in sex equality, a stance supported to date by the empirical evidence from socialist/communist societies. Whether the abolition of private property is even a *necessary* precondition to sex equality today is unclear.

The pursuit of ever-larger economic surplus is curvilinear in its effects on the division of productive labor by sex. As noted, the initial evolution from sustenance to surplus production typically entails the increasing participation of males in productive labor. In most sustenance societies, males constitute the "underemployed" sex; therefore, when additional labor power is needed to increase production, the males are available to provide it.

Among highly industrialized societies, the opposite phenomenon is evident today. Historically, in the West the initial transition from agrarian to industrial production sometimes brought females into the labor force. Males were busy on the farms while female labor was underutilized in the rural sector (Berch 1982; Easton 1976: 393). The first mill hands in the New England textile industry, for instance, were female, but this trend was short-lived. As males left the agrarian sector and flooded the factories, all manner of "protective" legislation pushed females back into the reproductive/private sphere of specialization, allowing males once again a near-monopoly of productive/public sphere roles (see Huber 1976). As will be evident shortly, even this short-term trend is not characteristic of societies currently undergoing industrialization, nor, according to Tilly and Scott (1978, chap. 4), did industrialization affect the extent of women's productive work in England or France.

Beginning in the late 1950s in the United States, and underway now in other technologically highly advanced societies, the trend is once again reversing. For all but the most unskilled, adult males are almost fully employed in highly industrialized societies, except for cyclical fluctuations. Nonetheless, continued pursuit of economic surplus (combined with further technological developments) has vastly expanded the economies of postindustrial societies in recent decades. The tertiary sector has mushroomed, providing millions of new jobs. As in earlier times, the sex which was "underemployed" provided the labor for the new jobs. Women, in short, have been literally "pulled into" the labor force in postindustrial societies by the expansion of economies beyond the ability of males alone to staff the resulting jobs (Oppenheimer 1970). This structural phenomenon, the result of the continued pursuit of surplus, largely explains the changes that postindustrial societies, and most notably our own, have been witnessing in the last decade in the status and roles of women. This same phenomenon spurred the emergence of a new feminist movement, as was suggested in the last chapter.

3.14. *If the pursuit of economic surplus exhausts the ability of one sex to provide the necessary productive labor, the less productive sex will tend to be pulled into further involvement in the productive sphere.*

As a more general proposition, this subsumes proposition 3.12, which can now be seen as a special case of a more general phenomenon. Likewise, proposition 3.13 is specific to one type of case. It too can be made more generally applicable:

3.15. *When the pursuit of economic surplus results in the increased participation of a sex previously "underemployed" in productive labor, the other sex will tend to experience a decrease in the extent to which it owns/ controls the means and products of production.*

It is apparent, however, that even in postindustrial societies a large percentage of adult females still specialize in the reproductive/private sphere, i.e., women as a category remain "underemployed" in the productive/public sphere and continue to provide a reserve labor force. Thus, sex stratification to a significant degree remains. Given the persistence of female disadvantage, it is likely that in the event that the economy begins to shrink and a significant part of the labor force can no longer be employed, women will be selectively chosen to leave the productive sphere and return to specializing in the reproductive/private sphere. For different reasons, the end of World War II resulted in just this phenomenon. Pulled into the productive sector by a shortage of males during the war, women were fired in massive numbers to "make room for the men" when males again became available after leaving military service (Chafe 1972: 135 ff.; Trey 1972).

It should be noted that the previous discussion implicitly assumes that the population size does not, in any major way, exceed the ability of the economy to absorb the labor power of at least one sex. Where extensive overpopulation exists, economic expansion may serve to give production sphere roles to heretofore unemployed members of the sex which is normally more involved in such roles, rather than increasing the participation of the other sex. It is therefore predictable that in many Third World societies today, which are characterized by high birthrates and overpopulation, economic expansion will not serve to expand the opportunities of women in the productive sphere, and therefore will not serve to raise women's relative status.

During the late 18th and the 19th centuries, many parts of the nonindustrialized world were colonized by industrial nations. The primary motivation of the colonizers was profit-seeking, i.e., the pursuit of more surplus. They sought cheap raw materials, food, and new markets. To meet these purposes, the colonized societies had to produce goods for export. Many subsistence societies were converted into producers of surplus or exchange goods. Horticultural societies were encouraged, if not forced to adopt, the technology and productivity of agricultural production. Moreover, on the basis of ethnocentric beliefs, the new technology was given by Westerners to indigenous males, who may never have worked the land. This left the female horticulturalists to continue lower-status subsistence activity, while men gained status through exchange production, or to withdraw from production altogether. The new occupational opportunities created by colonizers—in the mines, on large plantations, in the military, and in the cities—were overwhelmingly given to males, who thus became part of the modernized, Westernized sector of the economy and were in an advantaged position to dominate when independence came. In short, the division of labor changed in many cases of colonization, mostly to the disadvantage of women, because of the direct activities of the colonizers, the impact of technological changes introduced by the colonizers, and often because of the shift from sustenance to surplus production (Boserup 1970; Draper and Cashdan 1975; Etienne and Leacock 1980; Martin and Voorhies 1975: 298 ff.; Sanday 1981: chap. 7). It is interesting to note exceptional cases where colonization did not serve to reduce the relative status of women. In Java both men and women were recruited by the Dutch into export production, thus maintaining their equal economic contributions from precolonial days (Stoler 1977). Likewise, for similar reasons both the Tlingit (Klein 1980) and the Trobriand Islanders (Weiner 1980) did not experience a decline in the relative status of women with the coming of colonization.

The impact of neocolonialism on the division of labor and sex stratification is more subtle but depends on basically the same types of phenomena evident under colonialism. Neocolonialism entails the asymmetric relationship between economically and technologically more advanced and less advanced societies. The asymmetry is twofold. First, it is in the form of dependence of the less advanced society on the more advanced for markets for relatively inexpensive raw materials, foodstuffs, and labor-intensive finished goods. Second, it entails dependence by the less advanced societies on the more advanced for the provision of relatively expensive, sophisticated, manufactured goods and technology. According to dependency theorists, the effect of neocolonialism is general poverty for most members of the less advanced societies. Moreover, women, and especially working-class and poor women, typically fare much worse than their male class equals in such societies (Arizpe 1977; Boulding 1976: 104; Elliott 1977).

To export enough to begin to keep up with the costs of imports, such societies must do two things: maintain low wages in labor-intensive production, and become maximally efficient in the production of exportable raw materials and foodstuffs. The low-paid, insecure, low-prestige, labor-intensive jobs are open to women, usually young and single (e.g., clothing manufacture in Taiwan; cf. Kung 1976). Berch (1982: 184) reports the following 1976 wages for unskilled female industrial workers: Hong Kong, 55¢/hr.; South Korea, 52¢/hr.; Phillipines, 32¢/hr.; and Indonesia, 17¢/hr. Other positions in the formal economy often become the preserve of men who, under colonialism, had been preferred and trained for them and which, at any rate, sometimes require strength and/or mobility (e.g., military service, mining, and large-scale agriculture). Urbanization often outpaces industrialization in these societies. Since jobs are relatively scarce, women's opportunities are kept very limited, especially in white-collar positions, on the assumption that males need the income more (Papanek 1977: 16). The only other major economic opportunities for most women in these societies are those in the "informal economy" (Arizpe 1977; Chincilla 1977)—prostitution, street-vending, domestic service, bar-girl—which are low in status, security, and pay (and often are not counted in the GNP or employment figures), or as subsistence, rural horticulturalists in an economy that is increasingly urbanized and based on money. In any case, women are largely removed from, or prevented from entering, the central productive roles, if indeed they are able to fill any economic role at all. Vasquez de Miranda (1977), for instance, demonstrated the decline of female labor force participation in Brazil that has accompanied economic development (see also Saffioti 1978), while Arizpe (1977: 31) documented the increasing unemployment rate of women relative to men in Mexico. A recent conference on Women's Contribution to Food Production and Rural Development in Africa (Niethammer 1981) reached similar conclusions concerning this geographical area. Rapid modernization has served to decrease women's access to the means of production, as well as their access to cash, in part because of "increasing mechanization of food processing tasks, with profits going to men," in part because cheap imports are reducing the market for crafts locally produced by women, and in part because complex regulations involving imports are reducing their trading opportunities (see also Ellovich 1980: 94–96). In summary:

3.16. *The more dependent a society is on trade with economically more advanced societies, the more likely that females will be kept out of or pushed out of valued productive roles.*

Biological, Demographic and Locational Variables, and Work Organization

The remaining variables depicted in Figure 3.1 all directly impact the extent to which each sex participates in productive activities and the forms of their participation. In some cases the relationships to be discussed have already been mentioned in other contexts.

RELATIVE IMPORTANCE OF PHYSICAL STRENGTH/MOBILITY IN PRODUCTION

Because of the biologically rooted differences in muscle mass between males and females, where the most important or basic production activities of a society require extensive physical strength, males will tend to monopolize those activities.

3.17. *The more physical strength is required for productive activities, the less the involvement of females in productive roles will tend to be.*

The extent to which strength is necessary to production is clearly a function of the type of technology and production. For instance, while women could readily grow food utilizing a hoe, the transition to agriculture replaced this implement with the plow which, being heavier and furrowing more deeply, requires much greater strength. Conversely, by harnessing inanimate energy sources to machinery, the industrial revolution reduced the strength requirement of most productive roles, even in the agrarian sector of the economy.

Within a society, different productive tasks may often require substantially different degrees of physical strength. For instance, in hunting/gathering societies, gathering and pursuit of small game requires little; hunting large game with projectile weapons requires a substantial amount. In pastoral societies, herding large animals requires substantial strength and is overwhelmingly monopolized by males (Martin and Voorhies 1975, chap. 10); milking animals requires little strength and is frequently done by females. (O'Kelly, 1980: 134) Therefore:

3.18. *The more diverse the strength requirements of different productive activities within a society, the more sex-segregated those activities will tend to be.*

Recall from Propositions 3.6 and 3.7 that, in turn, the degree of occupational segregation is also linked to the degree of sex stratification.

Extensive (i.e., wide-ranging) rapid physical mobility is difficult for women who are pregnant and/or caring for very young children. For most of human history, most adult females were in one or both of those conditions. Productive activities such as herding or hunting large animals require extensive and/or rapid mobility. They are therefore most efficiently conducted by males who, unlike females, are not encumbered by the young of the species. Indeed, Friedl (1975) argues that the mobility more than the strength requirement of hunting explains male monopoly of these activities.

3.19. *The more extensive and/or rapid physical mobility is required for productive activities, the less the involvement of females in productive roles will tend to be.*

3.20. *The more diverse the physical mobility requirements of different activities within a society, the more sex-segregated those activities will tend to be.*

Martin and Voorhies (1975, chap. 10) analyze a sample of 44 pastoral societies. They point out that a common feature of all such societies is "the constant demand for fresh pastorage" (1975: 336), which, of course, generally requires mobility. In two-thirds of these societies all aspects of herding are assigned exclusively to males. In the other third, women do the dairying tasks. Moreover, when herding provides all or almost all of the food, i.e., when it is not supplemented, or supplemented only in small amounts by cultivated plants, females are absent from productive activities. Such societies are also the most nomadic. As cultivation provides a greater share of the food supply, the societies become less nomadic and women participate more in productive activities, especially plant cultivation (1975: 339–40). Friedl (1975: 58) also argues that herding is likely to bring people into competition and conflict with other groups, resulting in warfare. As warfare is a male enterprise, herding must, perforce, be male.

EXTENT OF CHILDBEARING/NURTURANCE AND
WORKSITE/HOMESITE LOCATIONS

Societies differ substantially in the average number of children born per woman, that is, in their fertility rates. At one extreme, typified by most industrial societies today, women average two or fewer children. At the other extreme, characteristic of many agrarian societies, average fertility may be as high as six or eight children per woman. It is obvious that the more children, on the average, women in a given society bear, the more restricted their physical mobility is likely to be, excepting cases where the infant mortality rate is extremely high. In addition, the sheer amount of time and energy required to produce and nurture numerous children may make it difficult for women in high-fertility societies to do much more than those tasks related to nurturance and domesticity. This assertion is likely to hold despite the fact that in low-fertility societies women tend to devote much more time to each child and do so for a greater number of years per child. In other words, societal definitions concerning the value of children and proper forms of parenting tend to change as average family size shrinks, leading to an increased investment of time and attention per child. This increase probably does not match the total investment made in larger families, however. Yet a simple proposition directly linking average fertility and female participation in productive activities is probably not warranted. The ability of women with a large number of children to participate in the productive sphere is undoubtedly influenced by the nature of production activities in their society.

The presence of several dependent children and/or frequent pregnancies would have relatively little impact on women's productive work if that work required relatively little physical mobility and required only a short attention span. Tasks such as gathering fruits and nuts or catching small game can often be done within a distance that young children can walk and infants can be carried. These tasks are also amenable to frequent interruption, a fact of life for those caring for young children. Likewise, horticultural work on plots near the domicile can be done by women in high-fertility societies. Agricultural cultivation, on the other hand, involves larger units of land which, therefore, are frequently located a considerable distance from the homesite. Moreover, constant interruption of plowing, especially animal-drawn plows, is less feasible than interruption of hoeing and spading. As noted earlier, hunting, fishing, and herding all involve considerable, often rapid, mobility and, it might be added, their success depends on uninterruptable attention for relatively lengthy time periods.

3.21. *The higher the average fertility rate in a society and the greater the distance between worksite and homesite, the less involved women will tend to be in productive activities.*

3.22. *The higher the average fertility rate and the more the productive activities require lengthy attention spans, the less involved women will tend to be in productive activities.*

3.23. *In societies where productive activities vary in their distance from the homesite and/or in the required attention span, the higher the fertility rate, the more sex-segregated productive work will tend to be.*

Propositions 3.21–3.23 speak to the *conjoined* effects of fertility rates and relative worksite/homesite locations, and fertility rates and required attention spans, on the extent and nature of women's participation in productive activities. Nonetheless, it is probable that the degree of separation of work and homesites has an *independent*, albeit smaller, impact on women's productive participation, as well. Even in low-fertility societies young children must be cared for, and it is everywhere defined as primarily the responsibility of women to do so. While it is possible to care for children collectively, as is done on kibbutzim and in some so-called communist societies, such care still falls overwhelmingly to women (see, for instance, Berch's description of China, 1982: 190–92). Very young children require a low caretaker-to-children ratio, thus involving many women in their care even when collectivized. Moreover, although such women are technically in the labor force and therefore can be considered as functioning in the productive/public sphere, they appear to receive low prestige for a work role which is maintenance-oriented rather than involved in the creation of surplus (Blumberg 1978: 112–16; O'Kelly 1980, chap. 10). For instance, as the birthrate increased after the first generation of pioneers, and women increasingly staffed the kibbutzim nurseries (as well as the communal kitchens and laundries) and deserted the fields, their prestige and authority decreased (see Blumberg 1978: 112–16; O'Kelly 1980: 308–11). Stated otherwise, the collectivization of domestic tasks still maintains a large proportion of women in roles that are not socially perceived as basic and important productive activities, but rather as extensions of domestic/private sphere roles. Therefore, even in low-fertility societies, to the extent that worksite and homesite are separated by substantial distance, as they are in agricultural as well as industrial societies, women's aggregate ability to perform productive roles will be somewhat curtailed. In passing, it should also be noted that except for hunting/gathering societies, low-fertility societies tend to be relatively wealthy compared to high fertility ones. That is, per capita income is usually related inversely to fertility rates. The result is that families in low-fertility societies often have more possessions, and more possessions require more maintenance, i.e., more domestic work. In these societies, a substantial proportion of women will spend at least some years either totally removed from productive activities or participating on only a part-time basis, as we see today in the United States and other industrialized societies. In societies where such activity is collectivized, the activities of some, not insignificant proportion of women will be permanently devoted to childrearing, freeing the rest for full-time commitment to productive activities.

3.24. *Controlling for fertility rates, the greater the separation of work and domestic locations, the lower women's aggregate contributions to productive activities will tend to be.*

In this and the last section the argument has been made that where considerable strength and/or mobility are required for production, where large numbers of offspring and/or substantial separation of work and homesites exist, and where work requires lengthy attention spans, women will tend to be less active in the productive sphere. These impediments should not be construed as necessary in the sense that any, or even all together, could not be overcome. Rather, it is a question of efficiency (cf. White, Burton and Brudner 1977). Given any, not to mention all, of these impediments to productive labor, it is more efficient to assign the productive tasks to males, as long as there are enough males to accomplish them adequately, and leave for women the domestic/reproductive tasks. Where insufficient males are available (e.g., during wartime) or where it is more profitable to exploit the productive labor of both sexes (e.g., under slavery), these "impediments" are ignored (see Blumberg 1979: 123).

Societies are rarely if ever characterized by women, on the average, bearing the biologically maximum number of children, but societies do vary in their ability to control fertility. Today, especially in technologically sophisticated societies, almost complete fertility control is possible, and the average real fertility rate thus reflects fairly accurately average desired fertility. Even in societies lacking intrauterine devices (IUDs), birth control pills, diaphrams, condoms, and safe abortions, other strategies often have been employed effectively to keep fertility down. These include late age of marriage, taboos against intercourse during particular (often quite lengthy) times, crude forms of abortion, coitus interruptus, life-long celibacy for some significant segment of the population, crude forms of condoms, and culturally prescribed or permitted homosexuality for some part of the population or during some stage of the life cycle. Thus, for instance, hunting/gathering societies, the technologically most simple of societal types, nonetheless tend to have relatively low birthrates and substantial spacing between children.

Under what circumstances do societies tend to restrict their fertility to a substantial degree? In simple societies it is probable that fertility control is used to prevent overpopulation, given available resources to sustain life. It is also likely that where women play major roles in production, fertility is restricted so as not to lose their contributions.

In more technologically sophisticated societies, average fertility is probably controlled for one or both of two reasons: economic conditions which cause families to feel they cannot afford many children; or enticing alternative roles available to women that preclude the raising of many children. The first instance is exemplified by the very low birthrates during the Great Depression of the 1930s throughout the Western world, and undoubtedly is also at work today in this era of rapid inflation. The second reason is the one germane to this theory and warrants a closer look.

After World War II the United States experienced more than a decade-long "baby-boom" that resulted in an average completed family size of more than three children. This coincided with a substantial reduction in employment opportunities for women, relative to the war years. By the end of the 1950s, as noted earlier, changes in the structure of the economy and labor force began "pulling" married women, and eventually mothers, into the labor force in numbers unprecedented in the history of the industrialized world (possibly excepting wartime).

Research in this country has consistently demonstrated a relationship between labor force participation and number of children of married women: the fewer the children, the more likely women are to be in the labor force. This relationship exists even among the most highly educated women with the largest amount of employment-related skills (Stewart, Lykes, and LaFrance 1982). While it is undoubtedly true that women with few or no children more readily choose employment, recent evidence (Cramer 1980; Stolzenberg and Waite 1977) appears to support the contention that women also choose to have fewer children when employed. In other words, to the extent that women have role alternatives in addition to motherhood, they will tend to restrict their fertility to avail themselves more fully and successfully of those alternatives. Indeed, even in technologically simple societies such as hunting/gathering ones, women's important role in acquiring sustenance for the community appears to result in wide child-spacing, i.e., relatively low birthrates (see, for instance, Howell 1976). Likewise, Murray and Alvarez (1975) note that in contemporary Haiti, women's important economic function as traders, which is seriously impeded by childbearing, affects their birthrates. Friedl (1975: 137) concludes from her study of foragers and horticulturalists that "the spacing of children and the allocation of responsibility for the care of the young are dependent on the subsistence tasks assigned to women in a society and not *vice versa.*"

3.25. *The more central productive work roles are available to women in a society, the lower the average fertility rate of that society will tend to be.*

SEX RATIO AND POPULATION DENSITY

Earlier in this chapter the issue of occupational sex segregation and the "replaceability" of each sex was discussed (Propositions 3.5–3.7). At that time it was tacitly assumed that sex segregation of any given task prevents replaceability by members of the other sex, i.e., the sex which does not usually engage in that task. Yet this is true only for tasks requiring skill and, more important in this context, it will hold only in the short run. Over time, members of the other sex can be trained to fill jobs normally not in their domain. Under what conditions might this occur? It might occur in situations of overpopulation, when members of a superordinate sex cannot find enough work and therefore invade the territory of the subordinate sex. More important in this context, it might occur when a chronic shortage of people of the "proper" sex exists, leading to a chronic shortage of labor for the relevant activities.

Such a chronic situation will exist when, given a system of sex-segregated activities, the sex ratio is skewed.

3.26. *In societies where one sex is not fully engaged in production activities, the greater the shortage of members of the other sex, the more likely the members of the less productive sex will be pulled into production activities (unless there is a condition of general overpopulation).*

3.27. *In societies where production activities are sex-segregated, the greater the departure of the sex ratio from 100, the more likely the sex in oversupply will engage in activities traditionally monopolized by the other sex (unless there is a condition of general overpopulation).*

The corollary to these propositions is that a sex in oversupply will not be readily replaceable by members of the other sex (see Blumberg 1979: 123).

The primary implications of these propositions for degree of sex stratification occur when males are in undersupply, that is, when the sex ratio falls significantly below 100. Under such circumstances, which occur primarily as the result of war and migration, females often face enhanced opportunities to enter production activities generally, and/or higher-status and -paying, previously male-monopolized activities. This, of course, will not occur in societies that have a general population surplus. As mentioned earlier, World War II had precisely the postulated effect on women in the U.S. (see Chafe 1972) and, it might be added, the U.S.S.R. In the latter case, along with most of eastern Europe, very high male mortality rates during the war resulted in expanded job opportunities for women long after the war was over (Scott 1979:

180–81), unlike the U.S., whose male war casualty rate was relatively low. For the U.S., a return to parity in sex ratio after the war resulted in a return to the *status quo ante* in terms of women's labor force participation. To reiterate, however, war and migration may serve only to reduce an existing oversupply of workers (i.e., overpopulation), and in such a case, regardless of how low the sex ratio might fall, females would not benefit in terms of increased access to productive roles.

It should also be noted that while changes in economic structure have resulted in greater labor force participation by U.S. women in recent decades, they have not successfully "invaded" heretofore male activities in great numbers (media coverage of "token" women not-withstanding). The labor force remains about as sex-segregated as before the influx of large numbers of women, and the vast majority of employed women work in a small number of traditionally female activities (clerical positions, retail sales, service jobs such as waitress and domestic, and selected semiprofessions such as teaching and nursing). This is exactly what could be predicted by the fact that the contemporary U.S. sex ratio is not skewed. No undersupply of males exists for activities traditionally monopolized by them (most forms of manufacture, wholesale sales, skilled trades, managerial and professional jobs). Job expansion has occurred primarily in the tertiary sector, and specifically in service-oriented and clerical jobs, traditionally the province of females.

It has been noted several times in this section that overpopulation may have ramifications for the division of productive labor by sex. Where there are too many people for the economy to employ, different dynamics may be expected than otherwise. Specifically,

3.28. *Where productive sphere tasks are sex-segregated, and where population density is sufficiently high that not enough productive/public sphere roles exist for members of the sex most heavily involved in that sphere, they will tend to engage in productive sphere activities traditionally monopolized by members of the other sex and to assume any new activities that may develop.*

In practical terms, the ramifications of this proposition are most applicable to contemporary societies with chronically high unemployment rates. Such societies, whether primarily agrarian, industrial, or in transition between the two, tend to be characterized by substantial sex stratification. Where males cannot find work, they may be inclined to invade positions held primarily by women who, because of their dis-advantage, lack the power to prevent it. For instance, as was mentioned earlier in this chapter, in the earliest stages of industrialization in the United States, females primarily staffed the mills, as most men were already employed in agriculture or commerce (Berch 1982). Increasing population—through natural increase and, more important, immigration—led rather quickly to their replacement by males. Likewise, in recent years in the U.S., shortages of jobs for college-educated males, along with a decreasing proportion of traditionally male, blue-collar ones, have resulted in substantial male incursion into such traditional female occupations as public school teaching, telephone operator, secretarial work, and social work (see Berch 1982: 204). Indeed, Jusenius (1976) concludes that to the extent that sex segregation has decreased in the U.S. labor force recently, it has been the result of men moving into traditional female jobs, not women moving into jobs traditionally filled by males. This process may also help to account for the phenomenon of rising female unemployment rates relative to male in countries such as Brazil and Mexico, which are characterized by high rates of population growth.

A Theoretical Digression

The contemporary U.S. literature in the disciplines of sociology and economics which addresses issues of income inequality tends to be divided into two theoretical camps: the Human Capital Approach and Split (Dual or Segmented) Labor Market Theory.

The Human Capital approach, exemplified by the work of Becker (1971, 1975, 1976), argues that different people and categories of people (e.g., males compared to females) acquire different skills, attributes, and work-related experiences that make them more or less valuable to potential employers. In turn, employers have "tastes" in terms of the social-demographic characteristics of people they prefer to hire and promote (see Arrow 1973; Welch 1975). As long as decision-making on the basis of such "tastes" does not interfere with profit maximization, employers will act in accordance with their tastes. Thus, members of those categories whom employers tend not to want to hire (typically women and racial minorities) must accumulate sufficient skills, educational credentials, personal and intellectual attributes—that is, human capital—to make it unprofitable for potential employers to discriminate against them.

This approach is seen by Dual or Split Labor Market theorists as "blaming the victim" by emphasizing faults or shortcomings among members of disadvantaged groups as the explanations for their disadvantage. Beginning with the work of Bonacich (1972; see also Freedman with Maclachlan 1976; Gordon 1972, 1979; Harrison and Sum 1979; Piore 1975; and Stone 1975) many sociologists joined a group of economists to argue that the cause of economic disadvantage is to be found in the structure of the labor market, not characteristics of disadvantaged workers. This theoretical approach generally divides jobs into two types: those in the primary segment and those in the secondary labor market. The first are characterized by good wages, advancement opportunity, decent working conditions, substantial autonomy from close control and supervision, and job security through "shelters" such as unions, civil service regulations, and professional monopolies (Freedman with Maclachlan 1976). The latter types of jobs are characterized by the opposite features. Once a worker is in the secondary labor force, movement into the primary is said to be very difficult. The characteristics of the secondary labor force shape worker characteristics, leading to frequent job changes (i.e., unstable job histories), and a lack of independence, confidence, and achievement orientation (see Averitt 1968; Doeringer and Piore 1971). In turn, such characteristics make them undesirable to primary sector employers. Women and racial/ethnic minorities disproportionately fill jobs in the secondary labor market, which explains why they are disadvantaged in income relative to white males (see Barron and Norris, 1976, for a similar analysis concerning women in Great Britain).

These theories have been developed primarily in terms of one highly industrialized society, the contemporary United States. Can one or both be accomodated by the theory being developed in this book? The answer is "yes" in terms of both approaches, which this author does not view as mutually exclusive explanations of female disadvantage.

In the last chapter it was argued that gender stereotypes create expectations concerning the relative abilities of males and females. Such expectations, in turn, can result in behavior predicated on them, such as employer discrimination for or against certain categories of workers. This addresses the employer "taste" variable discussed by Human Capital theorists and thus, to some extent the Split Labor Market issue of why women tend to enter the labor force in secondary segment jobs in the first place. Like the Split Labor Market theorists, the discussion in Chapter 2 also emphasized that people's behavior often reflects, or is shaped by, the roles in which they find themselves. Once in "bad" jobs, behaviors arise which make women less desirable for "good" (i.e., primary sector) jobs. As Barron and Norris (1976: 50) note: "Individuals who are confined to a particular sector of the labour market will acquire histories and attitudes which reflect their jobs. . . . These characteristics may then be seized upon . . . to justify . . . the confinement of certain workers to a particular sector of the labour market." In this way, a "circular process operates."

In this chapter several variables were discussed that may contribute to an understanding of why women disproportionately enter the secondary labor market. Because of their involvement in child-care in a context where work and homesites are typically far apart, women often absent themselves from the labor force, totally or partially, for a number of years, thus reducing their "human capital" in terms of experience, and current relevance of past education and skill development. Jobs which can be readily entered, left, and reentered, and/or worked part–time would tend to be those in the secondary labor market. Moreover, given their general domestic responsibilities, which are far in excess of those faced by males, jobs which require low levels of absenteeism, periodic geographical transfers, overtime work, travel, and in general a high level of commitment—many jobs in the primary labor market—might be seen by women, employers, or both, as unsuitable to them (see Barron and Norris 1976: 54–64). The traditional, highly sex-segregated fields that women disproportionately enter, whether by choice or because of a lack of alternatives, are typically "unsheltered" by unions, professional monopoly, or civil service regulations. These are, for example, nursing, retail sales, most clerical work, and many service occupations, and they are, by definition, part of the secondary labor market (Barron and Norris 1976). The lack of a serious imbalance in the sex ratio has functioned to enable white males to maintain a near-monopoly of the primary labor market positions, despite a large-scale increase in the number of women entering the labor market. Male jobs are by definition "protected," and would tend to go to women only in the absence of sufficient males to fill them, an absence that does not exist. Given the necessity or desire to enter the labor force, then, women are constrained by lack of alternatives to choose among those jobs traditionally open to them, which are disporportionately located in the secondary labor market, but which have expanded dramatically in recent years.

In short, both theoretical approaches shed light on why females continue to be disadvantaged in the industrialized world. More to the point, the approach taken in this book is congruent with both Human Capital and Split Labor Market theories. Moreover, the theory developed in this book has the added advantage of being relevant to societies that are not industrialized, i.e., it has a broader scope of applicability.

Conclusions

In this chapter six variables, or clusters of variables, were directly related to six dimensions of work organization, which, as often noted, are themselves interrelated. In turn, the ways in which societies structure their productive activities were directly linked to the degree of sex stratification.

The central thesis of the theory presented in this book is that the ways in which societies organize their production activities and, to a lesser extent, structure their families constitute the most important factors in explaining the degree of sex stratification. Women will tend to be most disadvantaged relative to men where they make minimal contributions to the most valued productive activities of their societies. In turn, the extent of their contributions affect the degree to which they own/control the means and products of production, and hence the level of their disadvantage. The degree to which women are readily replaceable as productive workers also influences the extent to which their labors result in commensurate rewards. In turn, their replaceability as workers is related to the extent to which production activities are sex-segregated. These aspects of work organization were explained in terms of several biological, demographic, and locational variables. The relationship between aspects of work organization and dimensions of family structure were also explored in this chapter. In the next chapter focus will be centered on the direct impact of family structure on degree of sex stratification, and of other variables on family structure.

4

THE FAMILY STRUCTURE VARIABLES

It has been noted several times that the three family structure variables, lineage, locality, and division of household labor, are collectively considered second in importance only to the work organization variables in explaining degree of sex stratification. In Chapter 2, the argument was made that the extent to which the division of household labor is specialized by sex affects the degree of gender differentiation. It was also argued that patrilineal structures are more likely than other lineage types to be associated with ideological/religious support for sex inequality. In turn, the social definitional variables affect the degree of sex stratification. In the last chapter, several dimensions of work organization were related to the family structure variables. First, lineage and locality structures were hypothesized as reflecting the importance of cohesive, one-sex, work groups. In turn, it was argued that lineage and locality structures affect which, if either, sex disproportionately owns/controls the means and products of production, which is directly related to degree of sex inequality. Finally, the division of household labor was seen to be a function of the extent to which females are involved in productive labor, and vice versa.

To the extent that the degree of sex stratification is a function of the work organization and social definitional variables, family structure has an important, though indirect, effect on the degree of sex inequality through its relationships to these variables. As will become apparent, it also has a direct relationship with the dependent variable. Only one variable in this theory has not already been discussed that is postulated as affecting family structure, namely, degree of social threat.

It might be supposed that the average number of children per family would be directly related to family structure. The logic of the argument in Chapter 3, however, is that the effects of this variable are mediated by one of the work organization variables. Specifically, fewer children make it more possible for women to engage in productive work, which in turn influences the division of domestic labor, and vice versa.

Wealth Transfer upon Marriage and Number of Spouses

In Chapter 1 wealth transfer upon marriage (bride price and dowry) and number of spouses (monogamy and polygamy) were explicitly excluded from the definition of the family structure variables to be considered in this theory. In passing, it was asserted that these dimensions might better be viewed as partial *indicators* of, rather than variables useful for explaining, the degree of sex stratification.

Bride price is the transfer of wealth (or labor) by the groom or his family to the bride's family upon engagement or marriage. Dowry is the opposite phenomenon; the bride's family transfers wealth to the groom upon marriage or engagement. The former is most often found in horticultural, the latter in agricultural and pastoral, societies (Blumberg 1978: 41). Recall that women play a central productive role in the former type of society and often little or virtually no productive role in the latter types. In addition, recall also that the degree of female disadvantage is substantially greater in agricultural and pastoral societies than in horticultural.

Bride price may be viewed as compensation to the bride's family not only for the upbringing of a valuable worker, but also for the loss of her productive contributions (Whyte 1978b: 100–101). The groom will, henceforth, receive the not inconsiderable contributions his wife can make to the family economy, as well as her offspring. O'Kelly (1980: 181) notes an interesting case in which bride price was practiced in an agrarian society, during the early Middle Ages in Europe. The practice existed at a time of a very low sex ratio, when the value of women as wives was relatively high due to their scarcity.

Dowry, on the other hand, may be viewed as an incentive to the groom to take an economic liability off the hands of the family of origin (Blumberg 1978: 41). Since the bride contributes little or no productive labor, she constitutes little more than an additional mouth to feed, body to house, and back to clothe for her family of origin.

Both practices appear most frequently in patrilineal societies and may be viewed as indicators of women's status as "property." In both cases the woman's offspring will belong to the patrilineage, so in neither case can it be said that the transfer of wealth "pays" for the right to the offspring. Nor can it be said that bride price signifies high status for females in any absolute sense. The two practices, however, have real and different ramifications for the ability of females to leave their marriages, hence for the treatment women are likely to receive from their husbands. Women whose families received bride price are strongly encouraged to remain in their marriages, since the family would otherwise have to return the wealth. Given their economic contributions, they may be treated fairly well normally. Dowry, on the other hand, constitutes a "cushion" for women to fall back upon in dealing with their husbands, since the threat to leave the marriage entails the threat that the husband will have to return the wealth received. Such a cushion may be very necessary to women who make minimal economic contributions to ensure that they are treated decently. Despite these very real ramifications for the lives of women, in neither case do such practices contribute to the relative productivity, hence status, of women. Rather, they reflect the organization of productive labor that makes of women either producers or mere consumers—"products" of greater or lesser value who require more or less protection from their husbands because of their economic contributions or lack thereof.

Most human societies practice either monogamy or polygyny; in contrast, polyandry is relatively rare, and often is found in conjunction with a very low sex ratio (see Leibowitz 1978: 132 ff). Schlegel (1972: 66) reports that about 17 percent of the matrilineal societies in her sample practiced polyandry, but suggests that this high percentage is unlikely to occur in nonmatrilineal societies. Moreover, even in these societies, she reports that "polyandrous unions are the exception rather than the common or preferred form of marriage" (1972: 88).

Polygyny requires the ability of a man to sustain several wives and relatively large numbers of offspring. It is most widely practiced in societies which are patrilineal, patrilocal, and horticultural. Martin and Voorhies (1975: 288) found in a sample of horticultural societies that 77 percent practice polygyny. In such societies women produce much of the wealth through their own labor. Men are motivated to have numerous wives to enhance their wealth (hence status), and numerous offspring to enhance the status of the patrilineage (see Blumberg 1978: 37, 41; Martin and Voorhies 1975: 236). The practice of polygyny is permitted in numerous pastoral and agrarian societies, which are also often patrilineal. In Martin and Voorhies's (1975: 288) agrarian sample, 31 percent practice polygyny, while 32 percent of their pastoral sample do so (1975: 347). In such societies, however, the vast majority of men are in fact monogamous or unmarried. Only the wealthy few can afford several wives, who are not economically productive, and the numerous offspring they produce (O'Kelly 1980: 158).

While the lives of women are most certainly affected by polygyny and by their place in the ranking of their husbands' wives, the *fact* of

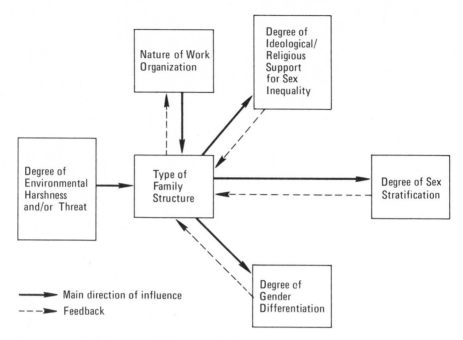

Figure 4.1   Direct Theoretical Linkages of *Type of Family Structure* **to Other Theoretical Variables**

polygyny or monogamy does not itself affect the extent of sex stratification. Number of wives is influenced by the type of economy, by the role of women in productive labor, and by the lineage structure of a society. But it does not in turn systematically influence the variables of interest in this theory. It was therefore omitted from the definition of the family structure variable.

Figure 4.1 depicts the direct linkages between family structure and the other variables in this theory. Most of these linkages, as noted, have already been discussed; only those not previously covered will be discussed in the remainder of this chapter.

Threat and Family Structure

In Chapter 3 it was argued that where cohesive, one-sex work groups are required, family lineage and locality structures tend to favor that sex. As horticultural societies evolve from sustenance to surplus-producing, males become more regularly involved in production, simultaneously reducing the number of matrilineal/matrilocal, and increasing the number of patrilineal/patrilocal, societies. It was also noted that in harsh environments, those in which it is relatively difficult for a society to gain its sustenance, there will tend to be a premium on cohesive male work groups, which attempt to exploit most efficiently the natural environment.

Physical environments vary in the ease with which human beings can produce what they need to sustain life. At one extreme are deserts and the tundra where, with anything but the most sophisticated technology, it is very difficult to "earn a living." At the other extreme are places of moderate climate and rainfall, good soil and vegetation, and extensive wildlife, where human collectivities with the simplest of technologies can readily survive. Obviously, the extent to which an environment is harsh is a function of both its innate qualities and the technology of the society residing within it.

By and large, in the preindustrial era, survival in a very harsh environment often depended on extensive physical mobility and/or strength. Pastoral societies (e.g., the Bedouin, the reindeer herders of northern Scandinavia) often existed in harsh environments where cultivation is difficult or impossible. Likewise, societies based heavily on hunting and fishing (e.g., the Eskimos) would be found in such environments. In areas somewhat less harsh, where cultivation is possible but difficult (e.g., because of very rocky terrain or extremely heavy vegetation), the physical labor required would be onerous compared to optimal cultivation environments. In all these cases male superiority in strength and/or mobility would tend to enhance their importance, relative to females, in productive activities. For example, sexual inequality is more extensive among Eskimos than among other hunting/gathering peoples (Friedl 1975; O'Kelly 1980: 90). Moreover, research on southwestern, coastal Alaskan Eskimos (Ager 1980), who live in a less harsh environment than other Eskimos, found females less disadvantaged than other studies of Eskimos have suggested. Likewise, the desert herding societies of the Near East are among the most extreme of all societies in degree of sex stratification. In a sample of 126 technologically simple societies, Sanday's data (1981: 159, figures recomputed) show that where the food supply is constant, 71 percent of the societies are characterized by the fact that females have political and economic power. Where the food supply fluctuates and no storage facilities exist to prevent famine, only 36 percent are characterized by female political and economic power. Conversely, in the former case, in only 16 percent of the societies do females lack both political and economic power, compared to 36 percent of the latter. In summary, a physically harsh environment tends to enhance the probability of extensive female disadvantage, probably in part because it increases the likelihood of a male-centered family structure indirectly through its impact on the work organization variables.

Recall that the variable *Degree of Environmental Harshness and/or Threat* was defined in Chapter 1 as consisting of two elements, one natural (just discussed) and one social. Social harshness refers to the extent to which a society, or its constituent parts, are involved in relatively chronic warfare with other competing human aggregates. This part of the variable is directly related to family structure. Warfare has been a male-dominated, indeed almost male-monopolized, activity in nearly all societies. It was already noted in Chapter 2 that militaristic societies tend to develop ideologies/religious thought systems emphasizing sex inequality. Males, being stronger, more physically mobile, and more biologically expendable, comprise the fighters, for any society that used its women to fight an all-male enemy would automatically be somewhat disadvantaged (Harris 1975). Moreover, excessive female deaths could seriously jeopardize a society's ability to reproduce itself. Waging war, whether clan disputes within a society or intersocietal warfare, is closely associated with high in-group cohesion, the willingness of most group members to accept orders from the few in authority, and a low level of internal conflict (see Coser's discussion of social conflict and group cohesion, 1956). Such conditions are maximized among life-long acquaintances related by blood. Patrilineage/patrilocality provide just such groups of males (see Denich 1974).

4.1. *The greater the degree of social threat, the greater the likelihood that the family structure will be patrilineal/patrilocal, and vice versa.*

Thus, for instance, Lenski (1970: 138) found that only 8 percent of hunting/gathering societies, in which patrilineage/patrilocality are relatively rare, engage in frequent warfare, compared to 82 percent of advanced horticultural societies, which, as stated before, are most frequently patrilineal and patrilocal. It is possible that social threat not only creates pressures toward patrilineal/patrilocal structure, but that family structure can affect the degree of social threat. Kriesberg (1982: 138) suggests that under conditions of matrilocality, warfare between communities could pit men against their own blood kin, with whom they no longer live, while under patrilocality men would, at worst, fight their in-laws. As a result, warfare is unlikely in the case of matrilocality.

It is likely that social and environmental threat/harshness are themselves interrelated (see, for instance, Sanday's discussion of the Yanomano, 1981: 45–50). Where the physical environment is harsh, intergroup competition over scarce resources is more probable. Working together, these two variables would constitute strong forces producing patrilineage/patrilocality. Therefore, it is not surprising that Martin and Voorhies

(1975: 220–29) report that *all* of the matrilineal/matrilocal societies in their sample exist in socially and physically safe environments.

Putting together the discussion from the previous chapter with this discussion, the following conclusions may be drawn concerning lineage/locality structures. Matrilineage/matrilocality exists only under very specific, limited circumstances: (a) in a nonthreatening physical and social environment where (b) the nature of production encourages cohesive female work groups as the key productive force. Patrilineage/patrilocality exists primarily where (a) the nature of production favors cohesive male work groups as a key productive force, either because of a physically difficult environment or an emphasis on surplus production; (b) the degree of social threat is high and chronic. Other forms of lineage/locality (e.g., avuncular) are viewed as transition stages between the two or as residual categories when the conditions favoring one or the other are not present or other conditions override these in importance.

One condition that overrides these in importance is a type of economy that places a premium on individual geographical mobility, which makes patri- and matrilocality impractical (e.g., an industrial society). Also, in economies where work roles are assigned primarily on the basis of formal credentialism, kin rarely work together. Thus, lineage becomes irrelevant to the formulation of work groups, even when cohesive work groups are required. And, of course, in some kinds of economies cohesive work groups are not the basis of production, which is more individuated. In addition, it is likely that as the dominant wealth form becomes fluid (i.e., money replaces land), and the influence of an older generation on the class or status of its offspring is limited largely to the provision of education (the development of "human capital"), a descent pattern that is bilateral maximizes a family's utility. When the economic prospects of one's offspring are determined primarily by the socialization process and their achieved education, one maximizes the family's interests by helping children of both sexes achieve their maximum prospects. What they ultimately inherit, if anything, will be far less important in most cases than what they achieve through marriage and/or job-related credentials. Bilateral descent permits the dispersal of familial resources in whatever manner the family believes will maximize its future interests. Moreover, it is often possible to increase daughters' resources (e.g., their access to education) without necessarily endangering sons' social class position. For these reasons, bilateral/neolocal family structures are almost universal in industrial societies. Finally, it should be noted that where nothing much exists to be inherited, e.g., in hunting/gathering societies, there is little reason to focus lineage on one side only. Martin and Voorhies (1975: 185), for instance, found that 62 percent of such societies in their sample are bilateral. In short, the propositions in which lineage/

locality constitutes the dependent variable implicitly hold constant, or control for these "other considerations."

Family Structure and Sex Stratification

LINEAGE

When a child is born, its biological mother is never in doubt, but the biological father is never absolutely certain. Where the lineage system ignores the father's family (i.e., in matrilineal and most avuncular systems), this second fact is not very important. In all other cases, but most especially in the case of patrilineage, the fact that paternity can never be established beyond doubt poses a fundamental problem: how can a man be sure that his heirs are really of his lineage?

The basic solution to this problem is often found in placing various restrictions on females past the age of puberty, restrictions not placed on males. Purdah, or the seclusion of women, is an extreme form of these restrictions. Chaperoning, veiling, and "modest attire" for women, such as long, loose robes, are less extreme forms. Social definitions that stigmatize women, but not men, for premarital and extramarital sex (the sexual "double standard") reflect the same phenomenon. In some societies (including some states in the United States, until recently) a husband could kill a wife found in the act of adultery, and it was considered legally justifiable homicide; the reverse (wife killing husband) was not defined as justified (Kanowitz 1969: 93). Stoning or killing an unmarried woman found not to be a virgin has also been permitted, even prescribed, in some societies (e.g., by the Old Testament and the Koran). All of these practices help to ensure that women will always be impregnated "legitimately," i.e., by their husbands.

It is interesting to note Martin and Voorhies's findings concerning a sample of 51 hunting/gathering societies (1975: 189). Only about one-quarter of them require female virginity upon marriage, and all but one of these societies are patrilineal. No bilateral, and only one matrilineal, society imposed such a requirement on women. In their sample of 40 horticultural societies, Martin and Voorhies (p. 247) found that 20 percent require virginity upon marriage, and all are patrilineal. Likewise, slightly more than one-third of the 23 pastoral societies in their sample require female virginity, and all are patrilineal (p. 350). Finally, among 53 agrarian societies, more than 40 percent require virginity, and this includes half of all patrilineal and nearly half of all bilateral, but no matrilineal, societies (p. 293). Considering all non-patrilineal societies in their sample, only 16 percent require virginity of women upon marriage, compared to 40 percent of patrilineal societies. Moreover, of all societies requiring it, 78 percent are patrilineal. Finally, of the non-patrilineal societies which require virginity of women upon marriage, all but one are bilateral; that is, paternity is of equal importance with maternity.

Although only indirectly germane to a discussion of the relationship between behavioral restrictions on women and lineage, Sanday's (1981: 106–9) findings are interesting. Among 101 technologically simple societies, she finds an inverse relationship between the number of menstrual taboos practiced by societies and the degree to which the sexes are equal: the less equal they are the higher the average number of taboos (1981: 106). Many such taboos entail restrictions on female behavior. Sanday also found that societies engaged in frequent warfare have a higher average number of such taboos than other societies (1981: 106). Given the earlier argument that patrilineage is associated with chronic warfare, it is likely that this type of family structure is associated with number of menstrual taboos, as well. Moreover, Sanday found an inverse relationship between the security of the food supply (a measure of environmental harshness) and the average number of sexual pollution beliefs (1981: 109): the more secure the food supply, the fewer the beliefs that female sexuality pollutes men. Again, given the earlier argument that linked patrilineage with environmental harshness, it is likely that this type of family structure also is linked to sexual pollution beliefs. In short, female bodies and sexuality are denigrated most often under conditions that are frequently related to patrilineage.

Recall from Chapter 1 that part of the definition of sex stratification concerns the degree of equality between the sexes in freedom from behavioral constraints. Societal practices that restrict women (but not men) in ways designed to insure known and "proper" paternity are, by definition, part of a system of sexual inequality.

4.2. The greater the emphasis on lineage traced through the father, the greater the restrictions on female (but not male) behavior (i.e., the greater the degree of sex stratification) will tend to be.

Where lineage is traced through only one parent's side of the family, inheritance will tend to flow primarily, if not exclusively, through same-sex family members (Blumberg 1979: 127). In a factor analytic study of 71 preindustrial societies, Gouldner and Peterson (1962: 21) found very high, positive loadings for patrilineal inheritance, patrilineal descent, patrilineal succession, patrilocal residence, and subjection or inferiority of women. Conversely, matrilineal inheritance and descent were strongly but negatively loaded on the same factor. As noted in the last chapter, one-sex lineage systems will tend to concentrate ownership/control of the means and products of production in the hands of one sex only, thus indirectly affecting the degree of sex stratification. Moreover, other forms of wealth will also be transmitted in the same way, thus providing a direct linkage between lineage structure and degree of sex stratification. But since matrilineage is found almost exclusively in non-surplus-producing societies, little wealth is usually available for transmission. Therefore, in reality only patrilineage is related directly to degree of sex stratification, as reflected in unequal wealth.

4.3. *The greater the emphasis on lineage traced through the father, the greater the relative wealth of males compared to females (i.e., the greater the degree of sex stratification) will tend to be.*

Combining Propositions 4.2 and 4.3:

4.4. *The greater the emphasis on lineage traced through the father, the greater the degree of sex stratification will tend to be.*

Where the degree of sex stratification is high, by definition males hold more prestige-conferring roles, as well as more authority. Under such circumstances, it is likely that they will view their male offspring as highly valuable, their daughters as of little worth. In turn, they will wish to confer upon their sons as much advantage as possible. A male-dominated lineage system permits them to do just that, as well as to emphasize their own descent from the more highly valued and advantaged half of the species.

4.5. *The greater the degree of sex stratification, the greater the likelihood that lineage is traced through the father.*

In short, lineage type and degree of sex stratification are mutually related variables, as depicted in Figure 4.1 by the feedback arrow between degree of sex stratification and family structure.

LOCALITY

Matri- and patrilocality force members of one sex to leave home, kin, and life-time acquaintances upon marriage, and to enter a world in which they are strangers. Moreover, while they are strangers, their spouses remain part of an integrated community of life-long acquaintances and blood ties. The uprooted, unlike their spouses, are therefore in an isolated position with relatively few resources at their disposal to influence their new community or even protect their own interests. In a system of neolocality, both spouses begin as equally isolated from kin and community support, thus reinforcing their dependence on one another.

Under conditions of matrilocality, the effect of keeping together related females of life-long acquaintance is to minimize female disadvantage. They form a cohesive group that can protect and enhance the interests of group members (Blumberg 1979: 127; Friedl 1975: 72). For reasons discussed in Chapter 1, females will not be more advantaged than males in such societies. But under conditions of patrilocality, females will tend to be relatively highly disadvantaged. As strangers, they have no friends, no allies, and no kin upon whom they can rely for help, at least during the early years of their marriage. They are almost completely dependent upon the whims of their husbands and his kin in day-to-day affairs. Conversely, their husbands are part of a cohesive group which can be relied upon to protect and enhance their interests (Friedl 1975: 67).

4.6. *If the locality structure favors one sex, that sex will tend to be more advantaged (males) or less disadvantaged (females) than under other systems of locality.*

Some Caveats

Family structure, especially in terms of lineage patterns, is vastly more varied and complex in reality than it has been treated in this theory (e.g., see Leibowitz 1978, chap. 4; Schlegel 1972, for a discussion of the complexities of matrilineage). Societies are not neatly divisible into matrilineal, patrilineal, and bilateral lineage, or matrilocal, patrilocal, and neolocal locality types, each being relatively homogeneous categories. The rich variety of empirically described family structures does not lend itself to general theorizing, however; a general theory requires substantial simplification. The propositions developed on the basis of this simplification are, after all, stochastic statements. A systematic test of the theory is needed to determine the usefulness of this particular approach. If, on the basis of the simplified types employed here, a significant amount of variance can be explained, then the approach is justified.

It should also be noted that one feature of family structure has been entirely omitted from discussion of this variable: authority or dominance. Although the degree to which males exercise authority within the family is variable, and which males dominate is also variable (e.g., brother or husband in matrilineal households; see Schlegel 1972), it appears that males surpass females in familial authority almost universally. The existence of ancient matriarchy, postulated by some feminists (e.g. Reed 1975), has yet to be demonstrated empirically (Van den Berghe 1973: 53). The extent of equality in degree of authority, both formal and informal, was listed in Chapter 1 as part of the definition of the dependent variable *Degree of Sex Stratification*. To have included this in the family structure variable would have been tautological.

The logic which related the work organization variables to degree of sex stratification can, however, be employed to elucidate the conditions under which intrafamilial authority will tend to be most unequal (or equal). Recall that females are hypothesized to be most generally disadvantaged where they contribute least to the (valued) productive activities of their societies and/or where males monopolize ownership/ control of the means and products of production. In turn, these variables are related to the family structure variables. The logical corollaries are that male familial authority will tend to be greatest where females contribute least to the (valued) productive activities of their societies and/or where males monopolize ownership/control of the means and products of production. Conversely, as females approach (or surpass) males in their contributions to, and control over, the productive sphere, they will tend to approach equality in the domestic decision-making sphere. Thus, also, familial authority will tend to be indirectly related to the three family structure variables, inasmuch as they are related to the work organization variables. It should be noted that the relationship postulated between women's productive contributions and family authority is supported by intrasocietal research on family decision-making. Studies in the United States (e.g., Bell, Chafetz and Horn 1982; Blood and Wolfe 1960) demonstrate that employed wives have more decision-making power *viz* their husbands than their nonemployed counterparts (see also Chafetz 1980a; Scanzoni and Scanzoni 1976: 313–14).

A final irony should be noted in this connection. In the last chapter it was argued that where females contribute least to production, they tend to monopolize domestic/private sphere work. Now it appears that, despite such monopoly, women in this situation are likely to have the least amount of familial authority. How are women in such a situation able to function? It is probable that they do indeed make most of the day-to-day decisions pertaining to household functioning and child-rearing. They are permitted to do so by their husbands, who may be little interested in such matters, as long as the husbands agree with the decisions made by their wives. But as Safilios-Rothschild (1970: 80) points out, "the relegation of decision-making power . . . does not mean lesser power for the relegating spouse. On the contrary, the relegating spouse enjoys more power . . . since he can orchestrate the power structure . . . according to his preferences and wishes."

A Theoretical Digression

Since the publication of Chodorow's book *The Reproduction of Mothering* (1978), there has been a lively and fruitful debate concerning the relative importance of psychological, social structural, and biological factors in the production and maintenance of male advantage and female spe-cialization in the parental role (see especially Lorber et al. 1981). Chodorow's overwhelming emphasis was placed upon the psychological dimension. She argued that the psychodynamics that result from the fact that females are the primary care-takers of the young in turn produce new generations of females, but not males, who have the capacity and want to "mother," i.e., be primary care-takers of the young. For males, the same process (i.e., having a female as primary care-taker) produces psychic predispositions that reinforce female disadvantage generally, and the particular economic and political structures characteristic of our own (and presumably other modern) society. Chodorow states:

> The division of labor in which women mother was responsible for the relegation of women to the home as home and work separated, and this division accounts for the sex segregation in paid work that produces income inequality. The ideology of patriarchy and the ideology about mothering arise from the very division of labor they are said to explain. Objectification and devaluation of women and expectations of total maternal investment themselves are products of a historically deepened association of women with the domestic sphere and with maternal responsibilities. This objec-tification and devaluation and these expectations *give cultural expression to psychological outcomes of being reared by women.* [Lorber et al. 1981: 508, emphasis added]

Elsewhere (Lorber et al. 1981: 502) Chodorow exhorts "feminists" to "insist on and understand the reverse" of the assertion that the structure of the economy and polity determines the structure of the family and the sex-gender system. Finally, she states that without understanding and psychodynamics of mother-daughter, mother-son and husband-wife relations, "you cannot understand how—male-dominant society and culture—are *produced*" (emphasis added).

From the vantage point of the theory developed in this book, and in keeping with Lorber's critique of Chodorow's book (Lorber et al. 1981: 482–86), Chodorow's argument is backwards: maternal investment primarily reflects, rather than initiates, the manner in which a society structures its economy and other nonfamilial institutions. From this perspective, the importance of Chodorow's work is in detailing the resultant psychological mechanisms that tend to reinforce the structural status quo.

Chodorow clearly does not deny the interactive process between the psychic and structural levels (see especially her statement in Lorber et al. 1981: 500–514). The issue is one of the relative primacy of psychological versus economic variables in explaining female disadvantage. The basis for attributing primacy to the structural, and especially economic, level is that in all societies women "mother," that is, function as primary care-takers of the young. But the structural features of societies, including the extent of female disadvantage, vary widely, which, after all, is the point of this book. The variable features of structure are simply not explicable by reference to the constant phenomenon of female mothering. The intensity of female involvement in the maternal role is variable, but it varies primarily in response to their involvement in productive activities. However, once a given pattern of mothering emerges, it undoubtedly reinforces the structure that produced it through its psychological effects on succeeding generations of females and males alike.

Conclusions

Family structure is shaped primarily by environmental forces and the structure of productive activities in a society. In turn, the family structure influences the manner in which productive work is organized. Together, family structure and work organizational variables constitute the major forces determining the extent to which females are disadvantaged relative to males. A series of variables—technological, demographic, and environmental—serve as the independent variables for the entire theory, and the next chapter focuses attention on this set of independent variables.

5

THE INDEPENDENT VARIABLES: TECHNOLOGICAL, ENVIRONMENTAL, AND DEMOGRAPHIC

Eight variables in this theory serve as independent variables: average percent of female life cycle devoted to childbearing/nurturance, degree of separation of work- and homesites, relative importance of physical strength/mobility in production, relative societal emphasis on sustenance vs. surplus production, degree of environmental threat/harshness, level/type of technology, population density, and sex ratio. Most have already been discussed as they relate to the social definitional, work organizational, and/or family structural variables. None is directly related to the dependent variable *degree of sex stratification*. What remains to be examined are the relationships among these eight variables, the focus of this chapter.

Physical Strength/Mobility and Production

In Chapter 3 four propositions (3.17–3.20) linked the variable *Relative Importance of Physical Strength/Mobility in Production* with the work organization variables. Two basic points were made: (a) the more physical strength and/or mobility is required for production activities in a society, the less females will tend to be involved; and (b) the more diverse the mobility and/or strength requirements of productive activities, the more sex-segregated productive roles will tend to be.

Figure 5.1 shows the direct relationships of the strength/mobility variable with other variables in this theory. The three relationships not

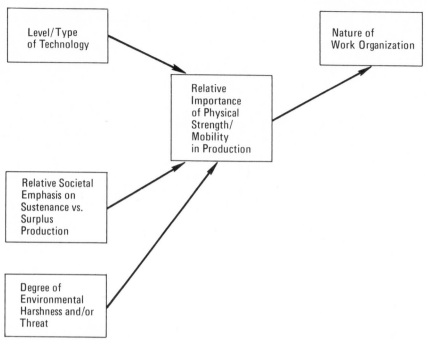

Figure 5.1   Direct Theoretical Linkages of *Relative Importance of Physical Strength/Mobility in Production* **to Other Variables**

already discussed depict a nonreciprocal impact on the strength/mobility variable.

As previously suggested, in situations of environmental harshness extensive strength and/or mobility are often essential to gain sustenance. Cultivation of rocky or mountainous terrain requires much greater exertion than that of flat, deep soil. Herding reindeer or camel in regions of sparse vegetation requires extensive, sometimes rapid, mobility. Hunting whale, fish, or caribou requires both strength and mobility. Of course, all these situations refer to preindustrial societies where production is tied intimately to the natural environment. Equally obviously, the type of technology employed will affect the extent to which environmental harshness is associated with requirements for extensive strength and/or mobility. Cranes and forklifts, operable equally by men and women, permit the lifting of heavy objects without regard to strength.

5.1. *Holding constant the level and type of technology, the more harsh the physical environment, the greater the importance of physical strength and/or mobility in productive activities will tend to be.*

Earlier, it was suggested that the effort to produce economic surplus might entail greater physical exertion, at least in preindustrial contexts. When sustenance-oriented economies evolve into surplus-producing ones, in the absence of major technological change, work tends to become more intensive and to involve members of the less productive sex more fully in the productive process, as noted in Chapter 3. It is also likely that work becomes more arduous. For instance, a horticultural society that embarks upon the quest for (more) surplus must clear new land; to increase agricultural productivity, with a relatively unsophisticated technology might entail ploughing more deeply and/or using (more) heavy draught animals, both of which require extensive strength. Therefore,

5.2. *Holding constant the level and type of technology, the greater the emphasis on surplus production, the greater the importance of physical strength to production tends to be.*

Moreover, the production of surplus is typically related to the creation or expansion of trade. Such trade requires mobility for at least some segment of the society.

5.3. *The greater the emphasis on surplus production, the greater the importance of physical mobility for some segment of society to trade the surplus.*

In a number of African and non-Hispanic Caribbean societies, women constitute the traditional traders (Boserup 1970: 88–99; Martin and Voorhies 1975: 239; O'Kelly 1980: 11–12). This occurs where the system of production places control of the means and products of production in the hands of female producers (e.g., in some horticultural societies). In such situations women do tend to enjoy extensive prerogatives (Martin and Voorhies 1975: 239; Mintz 1971). But it is probable that in the majority of surplus-producing societies, trade is primarily a male activity, the result of their typically greater role in producing the surplus, their control over the surplus, and the greater ease with which they can be mobile to other communities and societies.

In discussing the impact of environmental harshness and surplus production on the importance of strength and/or mobility to production, technology was held constant. Probably the single most important influence on strength/mobility requirements is the level and type of technology. In this theory technology is often not a linear variable; the extent to which a technology is "sophisticated" in its usual meaning does not constitute the important aspect of the variable. More sophis-

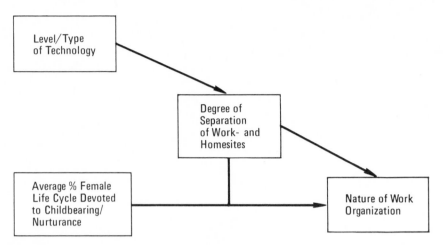

Figure 5.2   Direct Theoretical Linkages of *Degree of Separation of Work- and Homesites* **to Other Variables**

ticated technologies may, in fact, require more physical strength than less sophisticated ones, as has been demonstrated in the comparison of cultivation using a plow with horticulture using a hoe. In light of this, the only proposition that could be developed is tautological: the more a given technology requires physical strength, the greater the physical strength requirements for productive activities. Nevertheless, it is crucial to include technology as an independent variable in this theory, since technological change is probably a fundamental phenomenon that triggers changes in a variety of variables and thus indirectly, but powerfully, influences the degree of sex stratification.

Work/Homesites and Childbearing/Nurturance

In Chapter 3 the degree of separation of work- and homesites, and the average percentage of the female life cycle devoted to childbearing and -rearing, were related to the work organization variables. The argument was made that the separation of work- and homesites is both directly related to the extent to which women participate in the productive activities of their society, and related conjointly with the variable pertaining to the extent of women's childbearing/rearing responsibilities. In turn, women's participation in productive roles influences their involvement with children. These relationships are depicted in Figures 5.2 and 5.3 along with the remaining direct relationships of these two variables with others.

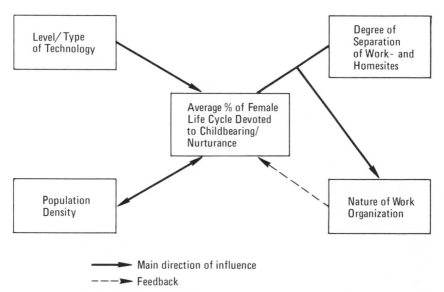

Figure 5.3   **Direct Theoretical Linkages of** *Average Percentage of Female Life Cycle Devoted to Childbearing/Nurturance* **to Other Variables**

Figure 5.2 depicts only one other variable influencing the extent to which work- and homesites are separated: the level/type of technology. Again, this variable is not linear, and no proposition is possible. Technological changes can alter the siting of work relative to home in a number of different ways. For instance, change from a horticultural to an agricultural method of cultivation often entails the use of larger plots of land, which may result in a greater distance between work- and homesites. The factory system of production, combined with the development of rapid mass transportation, entails an even greater separation of the two sites. Recent technological developments in the area of electronic communication may enable large segments of the work force in the future to conduct much, if not most, of their work at home-based computer terminals (Toffler 1980). Again, it is important to note that technological change can have a major impact on the degree to which work- and homesties are separated, but not necessarily in a linear fashion.

In Figure 5.3 two of the independent variables are related to the average percentage of the female life cycle devoted to childrearing/ nurturance. The technological impact is fairly limited in this case but exists in three ways. First, technological developments that successfully enable women to control their fertility (e.g., the pill, safe abortion, the

IUD, voluntary sterilization, diaphragms) can affect the birthrate. None-theless, societies lacking a sophisticated birth control technology have often had low birthrates, as discussed in Chapter 3. Indeed, the societal type characterized by the least sophisticated technology, hunting/gath-ering, is also characterized by low birthrates (Blumberg 1978: 8; O'Kelly 1980: 80).

Second, technological advance can affect the proportion of their life cycle women devote to nurturance in terms of infant feeding. Bottle-feeding frees mothers from having to nurture their own children, thereby helping to decrease the percentage of their lives females must devote to their offspring. Even in the absence of formula and bottles, women have found alternatives to nursing their own young. In some societies, very young infants were fed a thin gruel of premasticated food. Wet-nursing was widespread in preindustrial Europe and permitted one woman to nurture the offspring of several other women (see Tilly and Scott 1978: 132–33). Also, the average time during which babies are nursed can vary from a few months to a few years. The technologies developed in this century pertaining to birth control and infant feeding have, at the very least, facilitated that which women, when motivated by other factors to limit their commitment to children, did anyway.

Finally, technological changes that extend life expectancy can also affect the proportion of the female life cycle devoted to the young. Sanitation, food-growing and distribution, and medical technologies have all improved to extend dramatically the average life expectancy in most societies. This automatically expands the average number of years left in the life cycle after child-rearing responsibilities are completed, re-gardless of the average fertility rate.

In Chapter 1 it was explained that population density refers to the size of the population, given the ability of the environment and technology to sustain it. Stated another way, in a lush environment and/or with sophisticated technology, a greater number of people can be sustained than could subsist in the same space in a less hospitable natural enviornment and/or with simpler technology. In this sense, the variable *Population Density* only partly reflects the birthrate. If the environment and technology are held constant, however, the higher the birthrate, the greater the population density, at least in the absence of a high mortality rate.

Birthrate per se is not a variable in this theory. Instead, a closely related variable is used: average percentage of the female life cycle devoted to childbearing/nurturance. The difference between this variable and a statistical measure of average number of children per woman is important. Where children are highly valued and assumed to require substantial attention for a relatively prolonged time period, relatively low birthrates may still result in a relatively high investment of maternal life cycle in child nurturance. This is especially likely in postindustrial societies where children's futures are rooted heavily in the intellectual and personality traits they begin to develop (or fail to develop) at a very young age. High birthrates (in the absence of high rates of infant mortality) would almost necessarily involve an extensive investment, regardless of the per-child investment of time and effort. Lower birthrates may involve considerable maternal time and effort (as in many modern, industrialized societies), or may not (as is likely in many hunting/ gathering societies where children are seen as the collective responsibility of the society; see O'Kelly 1980: 101). With these caveats in mind, we now have:

5.4. *The higher the population density, the greater the proportion of the female life cycle devoted to childbearing/nurturance; however, the converse is not necessarily the case.*

5.5. *Holding constant the amount of maternal investment per child, the greater the proportion of the female life cycle devoted to childbearing/ nurturance, the greater the population density.* Or, combined:

5.6. *Controlling for maternal investment per child, the greater the population density, the higher the average percentage of the female life cycle devoted to childbearing/nurturance, and vice versa.*

It should be noted that proposition 5.6 verges on the tautological, or, at the very least, the trivial. The importance of this discussion is not in the resulting proposition, but in sensitizing us to the interaction of a series of variables: environmental and technological, attitudes toward the nature and value of children, and average fertility or birthrates.

Technology and Sustenance/Surplus Production

The technology available to a society, and the relative ability of a society to produce surplus goods, are intimately related to one another (see Lenski 1966). Indeed, according to Lenski, societal types are often defined precisely in terms of these two variables. His societal types, used in part or whole by so many of those who study sex stratification, are defined in terms that a given type or level of technology permits a society to produce a given proportion of surplus. That societies which are the same type tend to be similar in many other ways (e.g., the extent of both social or class and sex stratification) attests to the powerful influence of these two variables. Stated otherwise, many, if not most, of the variables in this theory tend to co-vary strongly with societal

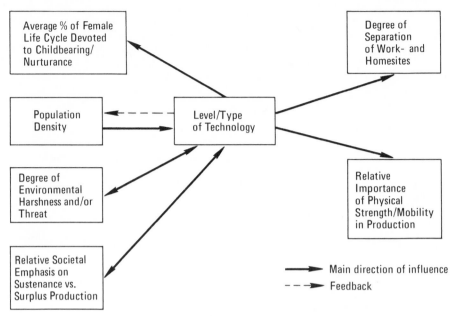

Figure 5.4   Direct Theoretical Linkages of *Level/Type of Technology* to Other Variables

types, i.e., level and type of technology and degree of surplus production. It is undoubtedly this phenomenon that has led researchers in the field of sex stratification (e.g., Blumberg 1978; Martin and Voorhies 1975; O'Kelly 1980) to use types rather than general variables in their explanatory schemes. Figures 5.4 and 5.5 depict the direct relationships of these two variables to one another and to the other variables in the theory.

Technologies vary in a linear fashion according to their efficiency; that is, the ability of and effort required by a people using the technologies to produce goods and services. Technologies limit the extent to which a surplus can be produced, but as pointed out earlier, a society may produce little because it desires little, not because it is unable to produce more (Blumberg 1978: 14, 35; Sahlins 1972, chap. 2). A technology may be said to be more sophisticated than other technologies when it permits greater productivity per person, regardless of the level of human exertion required, and/or when it permits the same level of productivity with less exertion. The advent of plow cultivation greatly increased per-capita productivity. On the other hand, the introduction of metal tools among hunters reduced the effort necessary to catch and butcher game, without necessarily increasing the total catch. Metallurgy, too, is uniformly

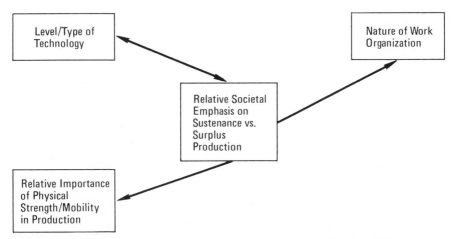

Figure 5.5   Direct Theoretical Linkages of *Relative Societal Emphasis on Sustenance vs. Surplus Production* **to Other Variables**

considered a major technological advance. Industrialization combines both attributes: less human exertion and higher per-capita productivity.

Technological development is often spawned by adversity or the perception of necessity, as well as by the desire to improve the quality of life. To the extent that a society endures substantial population pressure, impetus to improve the food-growing/gathering technology may arise (Blumberg 1978: 18–19). Communal survival threats from other societies (warfare) or a deteriorating environment may also spur invention. In turn, new technologies may help to alleviate the stress by increasing the food supply or rendering the collectivity less vulnerable to external threat.

5.6. *The greater the population density and/or degree of environmental threat/harshness, the higher the probability that more efficient technologies will be developed, which, in turn, will tend to reduce population pressure and/or environmental threat/harshness.*

5.7. *Assuming the desire to produce a surplus, the more sophisticated the technology available to a society, the greater the surplus it is able to produce.*

Figures 5.4 and 5.5 show a double-pointed arrow connecting these two variables. As Lenski (1966) argued, surplus production sets in motion the development of social class inequality. Unlike a sustenance-based society where the principle of distribution is the altruistic one of need,

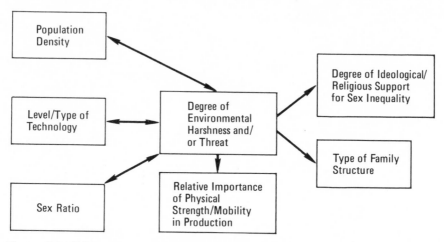

Figure 5.6   Direct Theoretical Linkages of *Degree of Environmental Harshness and/or Threat* **to Other Variables**

in surplus-producing societies an elite arises that expropriates the surplus. The prestige, power, and perquisites of that elite increase with their wealth, i.e., the size of the surplus to which they can lay claim. One mechanism by which they can enhance their wealth is to control more people. As numerous scholars, including Lenski (1966; see also, Sahlins 1982: Chap. 3), have noted, with increasing surplus come increasingly large and complex political forms. Another way of enhancing their position is for the elite to encourage further technological development, which can be used to increase the per-capita productivity, hence surplus production, of their subordinates.

    5.8. *The more surplus a society is able to produce, the more incentive the elite is likely to provide for technological development.*

    In short, technological development spurs surplus production, which enhances the status of a minority of societal members who, in turn, may be motivated to encourage further technological development.

Environmental Threat/Harshness

The degree of environmental threat/harshness has been directly linked to two of the three sets of intervening variables discussed in Chapters 2 through 4, and to the third via its impact on the strength/mobility variable. This variable constitutes one of the most important variables in the theory, although its major impact is probably confined to preindustrial societies. In Figure 5.6 it is also shown to be related directly to population density, sex ratio, and level/type of technology.

Without a highly sophisticated technology, physically harsh environments cannot support many people. Conversely, high population density can, over time, cause substantial environmental deterioration, resulting in the creation of a more physically harsh environment. Overgrazing, overcultivation, overuse of a limited water supply, and pollution of water or air are examples of this phenomenon. In the Middle East and in sub-Saharan Africa, land once amenable to cultivation has been turned into desert through human misuse. Some areas once heavily populated are almost deserted today.

5.9. *The more physically harsh the environment, the lower the population density will tend to be.*

5.10. *The higher the population density, the higher the probability of converting a non-harsh into a physically harsh environment.*

The higher the population density, the greater the competition for life-sustaining requisites and/or other scarce values. Such competition may exist within a society, or between neighboring societies inhabiting the same environmental niche (Harris 1974, 1975, 1977; O'Kelly 1980: 11, 137). Therefore:

5.11. *The higher the population density, the greater the degree of social threat will tend to be.*

Nevertheless, chronic warfare may well reduce population density through the death or capture of substantial numbers of societal members. Therefore, over time:

5.12. *The greater the degree of social threat experienced by a society, the higher the probability that population density will decrease.*

These four propositions may be reduced to two, which are processual in nature:

5.13. *The higher the population density, the greater the likelihood that the degree of environmental threat/harshness will increase.*

5.14. *The greater the degree of environmental threat/harshness, the lower the population density will tend to become.*

Environmental threat/harshness is also related to the sex ratio in a mutually interactive way (see Sanday's description of the Yanomano 1981: 45–47). In technologically simple societies, a high sex ratio can serve as an impetus to warfare, motivating males to capture women from neighboring groups (see O'Kelly 1980: 120–21). Their very involvement in warfare, however, is likely over time to reduce the surplus of males.

5.15. *The higher the sex ratio in technologically simple societies, the greater the degree of social threat will tend to be.*

5.16. *The greater the degree of social threat, the lower the sex ratio is likely to become.*

In Chapter 2 female infanticide was discussed. Under conditions of extreme environmental harshness, infanticide may be practiced to restrict the number of mouths to feed. Whether or not female infants are differentially chosen for death is a function of the status of their sex in a given society. Since environmental harshness and female disadvantage tend to covary, it is highly probable that societies in physically harsh environments that practice infanticide will selectively choose female infants (see also Harris 1974, 1975, 1977). This, in turn, will directly affect the sex ratio.

5.17. *The more harsh the physical environment, the higher the sex ratio is likely to become.*

It is interesting to note the combined effects of the interrrelationship of these two variables, as stated in propositions 5.15 through 5.17. A physically harsh environment tends to produce a high sex ratio (5.17) which, in turn, may spur warfare (5.15), which then reduces the sex ratio (5.16). A logical prediction, then, is that in some preindustrial societies warfare is cyclical, rising and falling in response to ever-changing sex ratios which, in turn, respond to environmental considerations. For example, in a marginal environment, a prolonged drought, resulting in selective female infanticide, might set in motion a process that would result in extensive warfare many years later, when the high sex ratio cohort reached maturity and its males sought mates.

The Demographic Variables

Only one linkage remains to be discussed and is depicted in both Figures 5.7 and 5.8 which concern the variables *Population Density* and *Sex*

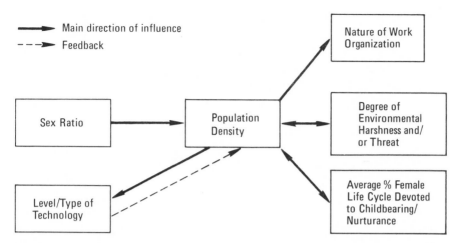

Figure 5.7   Direct Theoretical Linkages of *Population Density* **to Other Variables**

Ratio. Population density has been of relatively minor importance in this theory, affecting only three of the other independent variables and having only one, minor, direct relationship to a major intervening variable. Sex ratio, however, is postulated as directly affecting two of the three major intervening variables, as well as two of the independent variables. Sex ratio and population density are linked in an obvious way. Since only females can have babies, the total size of a society's population—the population density—rests first and foremost (although not exclusively) on the number of females in that society at a prior time.

5.18. *Holding constant the average fertility of females, the lower the sex ratio of the cohort in which the women are in their child-bearing years, the lower the population density at some future point in time.*

Conclusions

In this chapter the relationships among the eight independent variables in this theory were explored. They are not all equally important to this theory. The environmental threat/harshness variable is of major importance to explaining the degree of sex stratification, at least in preindustrial societies: it directly affects the extent of ideological/religious support for sex inequality and the type of family structure. Through its impact on the strength/mobility variable, it also affects the third set of intervening variables, which pertain to work organization. Likewise, sex ratio directly affects two of the three intervening variables, including

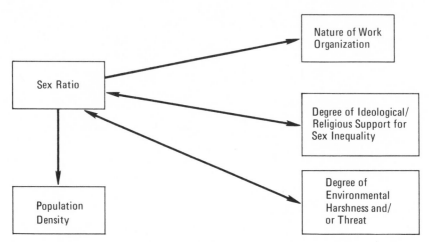

Figure 5.8   Direct Theoretical Linkages of *Sex Ratio* **to Other Variables**

the most important (work organization), as well as the ideological/ religious one. Five of the independent variables have direct effects on only one set of intervening variables. But in each case they affect the single most important variable in the theory, which pertains to the manner in which productive work is organized. These five are relative societal emphasis on surplus vs. sustenance production, average percentage of female life cycle devoted to childbearing/nurturance, degree of separation of work- and homesites, relative importance of physical strength/mobility in production, and population density.

Finally, despite the fact that the technological variable is not directly related to any of the intervening variables, and despite the fact that for most purposes it is not a linear variable and propositional statements concerning its role in this theory cannot be made, it is very important. It is directly related to four variables which, together, have a powerful effect on work organization. In fact, in industrial societies technological change can directly affect the work organizational variables because of the sex-segregated nature of productive roles. Entire categories of jobs, filled overwhelmingly by members of one sex, can be deskilled or even eliminated by technological change (e.g., see Hacker 1982). Given the impact (albeit indirect) of technology on the work organization variables, it is probable that changes in the dependent variable *Degree of Sex Stratification* are often triggered *primarily* by technological changes. Moreover, it is clear that cross-societal differences in degree of sex stratification are highly related to societal types, as defined by technological base. To assert that level/type of technology ultimately constitutes the "engine" which "drives" social systems and produces characteristic systems of sex stratification (among other phenomena) is in keeping with a long social scientific tradition. As Gouldner and Peterson note:

> A long line of social theorists from Saint-Simon through Marx, Ogburn, and anthropologists such as Childe, White, Steward, and Goldschmidt have, although stating their nominations variously, commonly stressed the influence of technology. [Gouldner and Peterson 1962: 10]

Moreover, their own factor analytic study of 71 preindustrial societies led Gouldner and Peterson to conclude "that, of all the various factors influencing sociocultural outcomes, technology is *relatively the most important*" (p. 57, emphasis in original).

In the next and final chapter a summary will be presented in terms of a propositional inventory.

6

SUMMARY AND CONCLUSIONS

The intent of this book has been to present a macro-structural theory to explain the degree of sex stratification cross-culturally and historically. Variables concerned with the degree to which societal members *perceive* female disadvantage and/or *evaluate* the sex stratification system as inequitable have been omitted intentionally. It is my contention that substantial inequities can and do exist without their being perceived and/or evaluated negatively by the victims of the system. Indeed, the disadvantaged may actually fear change, believing that change might make their situation worse (e.g., see Deaver's analysis of Saudi women, 1980: 39–40). It would require another theoretical exercise to explain the conditions under which the disadvantaged develop "class consciousness," although a few suggestions concerning this issue were made in Chapter 2.

A multivariate theory requires a multivariate test. Many of the propositions developed in Chapters 2 through 5 hold other variables constant. Virtually all of the propositions do so implicitly. Since the different variables are not all equally important to explaining the dependent variable, only a multivariate analysis can sort out which are empirically the most important and which are of limited impact, although the relative explanatory importance of the variables has been suggested in the presentation of this theory. To aid the testing process a summary of the theory follows, presented as a propositional inventory. Some of the propositions deemed of minor relevance will be omitted. Included are all that concern the relationships of intervening variables with the dependent variable, and those which link the independent variables to the intervening ones. Only a few others are included, which relate some of the independent variables to others. The propositions will begin with the independent variables and conclude with the dependent. In parentheses after each proposition is the number that appeared earlier in the text. Propositions will be grouped in terms of their *dependent variables*.

Propositional Inventory

Sex Ratio:

The greater the degree of ideological/religious support for sex in-equality, the higher the sex ratio will tend to be, under conditions of fundamental scarcity of life-sustaining requisites (2.11).

The greater the degree of physical and/or social threat/harshness, the lower the sex ratio is likely to become (5.16 and 5.17).

Degree of Environmental Threat/Harshness:

The higher the population density, the greater the likelihood that the degree of environmental threat/harshness will increase (5.13).

The higher the sex ratio in technologically simple societies, the greater the degree of social threat will tend to be (5.15).

Relative Importance of Physical Strength/Mobility to Production:

Holding constant the level and type of technology, the more harsh the physical environment, the greater the importance of physical strength/ mobility to production activities will tend to be (5.1).

Holding constant the level and type of technology, the greater the emphasis on surplus production, the greater the importance of physical strength to production will tend to be (5.2).

The greater the emphasis on surplus production, the greater the importance of physical mobility for some segment of society, in order to trade the surplus (5.3).

Relative Emphasis on Sustenance vs. Surplus Production:

Assuming a desire to produce a surplus, the more sophisticated the technology available to a society, the greater the surplus it is able to produce (5.7).

Average Proportion of Female Life Cycle Devoted to Childbearing/Nurturance:

The more central, productive work roles are available to women, the lower the average fertility rate (hence proportion of female life cycle devoted to children) of that society will tend to be (3.25).

Degree of Gender Differentiation:

The greater the degree of sex stratification, the greater the degree of gender differentiation will tend to be (2.5).

The more specialized the division of labor in the family and/or the division of productive labor, the more the sexes will tend to be distin-guished by general behavioral differences (and vice versa), and therefore the greater the degree of gender differentiation will tend to be, and vice versa (2.3 and 2.4).

The greater the degree of ideological/religious support for sex inequality, the greater the degree of gender differentiation will tend to be and vice versa (2.8).

Degree of Ideological/Religious Support for Sex Inequality:
The greater the degree of sex stratification, the greater the degree of ideological/religious support for sex inequality will tend to be (2.10).

The greater the departure of societal sex ratios from parity, the more likely the degree of ideological/religious support for sex inequality will be stronger if they are below 100, and weaker if they are above 100 (2.12).

The more a society engages in warfare (i.e., the greater the social threat), the greater its ideological/religious support for sex inequality will tend to be (2.13).

The more females contribute to the productive efforts of their society, and the more they control the means and products of production, the less the degree of ideological/religious support for sex inequality will tend to be (2.14).

Patrilineal societies will tend to have a higher degree of ideological/religious support for sex inequality than those characterized by other lineage forms, and vice versa (2.15).

Family Structure: Lineage and Locality:
The more the productive activities of a society enhance the importance of cohesive work groups comprised of one sex, the more likely the lineage patterns will flow through that sex and the locality patterns will maintain physical proximity of related members of that sex (3.8).

The greater the degree of social threat, the greater the likelihood that family structure will be patrilineal/patrilocal, and vice versa (4.1).

Family Structure: Division of Domestic Labor:
The greater the contributions made by females to productive/public sphere activities, the greater the contributions made by males to reproductive/private sphere activities will tend to be, and vice versa (3.11; see also 3.10).

Work Organization: Extent of Female Contribution to Production Activities:
The more physical strength and/or extensive/rapid physical mobility are required for production activities, the less the involvement of females in productive roles will tend to be (3.17 and 3.19).

Where one sex is not fully engaged in productive activities, the greater the shortage of members of the other sex, the more likely the members of the less productive sex will be pulled into productive activities (unless there is a condition of general overpopulation) (3.26).

If the pursuit of economic surplus exhausts the ability of one sex to provide the necessary labor, the less productive sex will tend to be pulled into further involvement in the productive sphere (3.14).

The higher the average fertility rate (hence proportion of female life cycle devoted to children) and the more the productive activities require lengthy attention spans, the less involved women will tend to be in production activities (3.22).

The higher the average fertility rate (hence proportion of female life cycle devoted to children) and the greater the distance betweeen work- and homesites, the less involved women will tend to be in productive activities (3.21).

Work Organization: Degree of Sex Segregation:

In societies where productive activities are highly sex-segregated, the greater the departure of the sex ratio from 100, the more likely the sex in oversupply will engage in activities traditionally monopolized by the other sex (unless there is a condition of general overpopulation). (3.27).

Where productive sphere tasks are sex-segregated and where population density is sufficiently high that not enough productive/public sphere roles exist for members of the sex most heavily involved in that sphere, they will tend to engage in productive sphere activities traditionally monopolized by members of the other sex and to assume any new activities that may develop (3.28).

In societies where productive activities vary in their distance from the homesite and/or in the required attention span, the higher the fertility rate (hence proportion of female life cycle devoted to children) the more sex-segregated productive work will tend to be (3.23).

The more diverse the physical strength and/or mobility requirements of different productive activities within a society, the more sex-segregated these activities will tend to be (3.18 and 3.20).

Work Organization: Replaceability:

The greater the occupational segregation by sex, the less males will tend to be able to replace females (3.6).

Work Organization: Ownership/Control of the Means and Products of Production:

When the pursuit of economic surplus results in the increased particpation of a sex previously "underemployed" in productive labor, the other sex will tend to experience a decrease in the extent to which it owns/controls the means and products of production (3.15).

Where lineage and locality structures reflect a one-sex bias, that sex will tend to disproportionately own/control the means and products of production (3.9).

Degree of Sex Stratification:

The greater the degree of gender differentiation, the greater the degree of ideological/religious support for sex inequality and therefore the greater the degree of sex stratification will tend to be (2.9).

The greater the emphasis on lineage traced through the father, the greater the degree of sex stratification will tend to be, and vice versa (4.4 and 4.5).

If the locality structure favors one sex, that sex will tend to be more advantaged (males) or less disadvantaged (females) than under other systems of locality (4.6).

The greater the involvement of females in the most important (highly valued) productive roles in their societies, the less the degree of sex stratification will tend to be, and vice versa (3.4).

In the absence of a surplus of potential female workers, the greater the occupational segregation by sex, the less the degree of sex stratification will tend to be (3.7).

The more replaceable women workers are, the greater the degree of sex stratification will tend to be (3.5).

The more males disproportionately own/control the means and products of production, the greater the degree of sex stratification will tend to be (3.1).

Theoretical Variables and Societal Types

In Chapters 1 and 5 the point was made that many, if not most, scholars who investigate sex stratification employ societal types as the major part of their organizing framework. Such types are usually defined in terms of technological base and associated dominant economic activity. As stated in the last chapter, societal ability to produce surplus is a closely related phenomenon, which is often included as part of the defining characteristics of the types. The point was also made that many of the variables that constitute this theory tend to co-vary strongly with each other and with societal types.

Figure 6.1 depicts the estimated values of most of the theoretical variables by societal type. *Level and Type of Technology* and *Relative Emphasis On Sustenance vs. Surplus Production* are omitted, since they constitute the main bases for defining societal types. *Sex Ratio* is also omitted because it is generally omitted from the relevant literature, and to estimate its values across societal types is impossible. Finally, *Population Density* is omitted because, as used in this theory, it automatically controls for level of technology. In its more usual meaning—number of people per areal unit—it varies directly with technological sophistication, hence societal type. All other variables in this theory are listed in Figure

Figure 6.1 Theoretical Variables and Societal Types

	Societal Types						
Theoretical Variables	Hunting/ Gathering	Simple Horticultural	Advanced Horticultural	Pastoral	Agrarian	Early Industrial	Post-industrial
1. Degree of Sex Stratification	very low	low	medium to high	very high	very high	high	medium to low
2. Degree of Ideological/ Religious Support for Sex Inequality	none to low	none to low	medium to high	very high	very high	high to very high	medium to low
3. Degree Gender Differentiation	low to medium	medium	medium to high	very high	very high	very high	medium to low
4. Family Structure a. Lineage/Locality	mixed; heavily neolocal/ bilateral	mixed; matrilineal/ matrilocal found only here	heavily patrilocal/ patrilineal	heavily patrilocal/ patrilineal	mostly neolocal/ bilateral	neolocal/ bilateral	neolocal/ bilateral
b. Division of Labor	medium to high male involvement	low to medium male involvement	low male involvement	female monopoly	female monopoly	female monopoly	low to medium male involvement
5. Work Organization a. Extent of Female Involvement	very high	very high	very high	very low	very low	low to medium	medium to high
b. Ownership/ Control	equal	equal to female control	mostly male control	male monopoly	male monopoly	mostly male control	male control but tending toward equal
c. Sex Segregation	very high	very high	high	very high	very high	high	medium
6. % Female Life cycle Devoted to Children	medium	high	high	high to very high	very high	high	medium to low
7. Separation of Work/ Homesites	medium to high	very low	very low	medium to very high	medium to very high	high to very high	high to very high
8. Importance of Strength/ Mobility	medium to very high	medium to low	medium to low	high to very high	none to very high	low	very low
9. Degree of Environmental Harshness and/or Threat	none to very high	none to low	medium to very high	high to very high	none to very high	low	low to very low

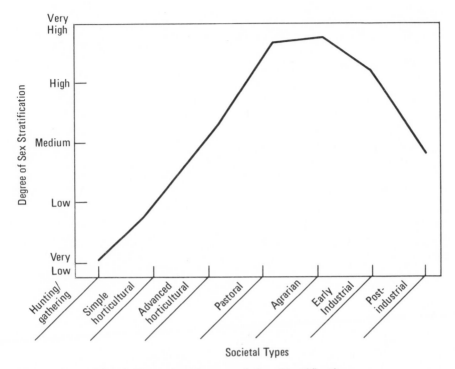

Figure 6.2   Societal Types by Degree of Sex Stratification

6.1 and, on the basis of the discussions in Chapters 1 through 5 and the literature on which they were based, values are estimated by societal types. In at least a few cases, these estimates are little more than educated guesses. The seven societal types used reflect those most commonly employed in the literature. For instance, most are used by Lenski (1966) in discussing social stratification. Nielsen (1978) uses all but the distinction of two types of horticultural societies. O'Kelly (1980) employs all of these types plus some others. Martin and Voorhies (1975) use this same typology, but only imply the distinction among the two horticultural types and do not distinguish two industrial types; Etienne and Leacock (1980: 8) also use the same types without distinguishing levels of horticultural or industrial societies.

One purpose of Figure 6.1 is to demonstrate graphically the substantial extent to which the theoretical variables do indeed tend to co-vary with one another and with societal types. Figure 6.2 depicts the direct relationship between societal types and degree of sex stratification, as represented in row 1 of Figure 6.1. It is interesting to note that the shape of this curve is essentially the same as a curve that could be drawn to depict Lenski's (1966) conclusions about the degree of social (class) stratification by societal types. Likewise, Etienne and Leacock argue:

> there is a rough correlation between the position of women vis-à-vis men and the degree of socioeconomic inequality in a society as a whole. This does not mean that female inequality follows from the development of class differences generally; instead, it is our understanding that the origins of both socioeconomic and sexual hierarchy are inextricably bound together. . . . the *relations set up among people* as they produce, distribute, exchange, and consume the goods upon which they live . . . are crucial for understanding socioeconomic and sexual hierarchies. [1980: 8]

This approach is further buttressed by Youssef and Hartley's (1979) research on 80 nations. After examining a number of demograhic, educational, and employment variables, they conclude with reference to the status and roles of women that "dissimilarities . . . are found to be greatest for different levels of industrialization, rather than by Western vs. Socialist bloc economic ideology" (1979: 93). Likewise, in a study of 61 contemporary societies with populations in excess of two million, Semyonov (1980) found that inequity of income was the only variable associated with the proportion of females in the labor force: the greater the inequality, the lower the percentage of females in the labor force. Income inequality is strongly and negatively related to level of industrialization. Therefore, it is not surprising that Semyonov (1980: 537) found a .525 correlation between percentage of females in the labor force and level of industrialization, as measured by per-capita energy consumption.

It is also important to note in Figure 6.1 that there is not complete co-variance, and this fact constitutes the major reason why theoretical development requires the use of general variables rather than societal types. If there were perfect co-variance, all the variables could be represented by curves similar to that in Figure 6.2, which is not the case. For instance, the sex segregation (5c), work/homesite location (7), strength/mobility (8), environmental threat/harshness (9), and lineage/ locality structure (4a) variables have different curves from that depicted in Figure 6.2. Some of the curves, e.g., the ideological/religious variable (2), are very similar to that depicted; others are similar but more "flat," e.g., degree of gender differentiation (3). In short, the theoretical variables stand in somewhat different relationships to the types of societies, reflecting the facts that they are of differential importance in explaining the dependent variable, and that some are important only in conjunction with others. Finally, it is important to note that there is considerable within-type variation on many, if not most, of the variables, as reflected both in Figure 6.1 and in the corpus of ethnographic studies of individual societies (see, for example, Etienne and Leacock 1980: 8).

As stated at the outset of this book, *types describe; they do not explain.* This work has been devoted to an attempt to discover what variables, while tending to be associated with societal types, can be employed to explain the degree to which females are disadvantaged.

More on Constants and Variables

This book began with the assertion that the conceptual variable *Degree of Sex Stratification* is comprised of two distinct empirical aspects, a constant and a variable. The constant is that females are never more advantaged than males; the variable is that the extent of comparative female disadvantage ranges from practically none to very extensive. The theory developed in this book has been an attempt to explain the empirically variable portion of the conceptual variable. Moreover, the logic of this theory can also be used to shed light upon the constant aspect of the dependent variable.

Chapter 1 offered a brief explanation of the empirically constant finding that nowhere are women, considered categorically, systematically more advantaged than men. The theory posits that the prime determinants of the relative statuses of the two sexes are several aspects of the way societies organize their productive activities. Those who own/control the means and products of production, and/or who engage in the most valued productive activities, will be more advantaged. The extent to which one sex surpasses the other in ownership/control of the means and products of production reflects the nature and extent of their own contributions to production and/or the lineage/locality structures of the society.

Most productive activities (and warfare, as well) involve people in extrafamilial alliances and exchange networks, especially to the extent that they produce a surplus and control the products of their labor. The contacts and mutual obligations that result from extradomestic or public sphere activities can result in potential power bases, prestige, indeed, access to a variety of resources not obtainable any other way (see Friedl 1975). The demographic, technological, and environmental factors that influence the degree to which the sexes participate in public vs. private sphere activities thus stand at the root of the degree of sex stratification and disadvantage.

In all societies most women spend at least some of their time and energy in reproductive/domestic sphere activities. The role of men in this sphere is highly variable, and in some societies their commitments approach zero: nowhere do men as a category specialize in or monopolize such activities. Conversely, nowhere do women as a category specialize in and monopolize the productive/public sphere activities. Therefore, women either perform roles in both spheres or only the reproductive/ domestic; men either perform roles in both spheres or only the productive/ public. Specialization in the productive/public sphere undergirds superior advantage and, conversely, specialization in the reproductive/domestic forms the basis of extensive disadvantage. Since males as a category never specialize in the reproductive/domestic, and females as a category never specialize totally in the productive/public sphere, females are never more advantaged than males. Moreover, it is unlikely that future societies will be formed in which males are disadvantaged relative to females, barring perhaps some brave new world of test-tube babies. Still, sexual equality is possible and has existed in some human societies.

A CAVEAT: THE ROLE OF PHYSICAL COERCION

In the large corpus of speculative work on the origins of female disadvantage relative to males, physical force has often played a key role. The fact that males are larger and stronger than females and capable of raping them is often viewed as important for explaining the origin and/or the continuation of systems of sexual inequality (see for instance, Brownmiller 1975; Bullough 1974; Collins 1972 and 1975; Goldberg 1973; Martin and Voorhies's review of 19th-century thought on the subject, 1975: 146–55). This variable has not been included in this theory for four reasons. First, male superiority in size and strength is relatively *constant* across time and space. Logically, one cannot explain a variable by reference to a constant, and this theory represents an attempt to explain a variable (see Sanday 1981: 184).

Second, it appears very inconsistent to argue that one form of stratification, but no others, results from size/strength differences. In discussions of social class inequality, caste systems, even systems of slavery, no one argues that superior status accrues to larger, stronger males who dominate shorter, weaker males; no one uses physical size or strength as an indicator of socioeconomic status. Why, then, should one form of stratification (sex) be treated as radically unlike all other forms? After all, the size/strength differences between the largest and smallest males are at least as great, if not greater, than the average differences between males and females.

Third, in terms of this theory, the concept of force is imbedded in the dependent variable itself. Recall that one suggested dimension of degree of sex stratification pertained to the extent to which the sexes are equally free from assaults by others. Another dimension was equality of formal power. Formal power in most societies, at least today, is state power, and states are characterized by a monopoly of the legitimate use of coercion. Yet another suggested dimension concerned informal power. The use or threat of force among family members, for instance, is one type of informal power. In short, in this theory, to the extent that sexual inequality exists, one of its many possible manifestations or dimensions is that women are more frequently the targets of male physical coercion than vice versa. Thus, while superior male strength is a constant, male *use* of force is a variable. It is altogether likely that this manifestation of inequality is related to other dimensions of inequality (see Blumberg 1979: 132), but that has not been the subject of this book. Indeed, in Chapter 1 further empirical and theoretical efforts to link the various dimensions of inequality were specifically called for.

Finally, force was included along with other dimensions of inequality rather than as an explanatory variable in the theory because of a set of assumptions I make about human beings and the nature of human societies. I believe that humans are essentially, meaning genetically, a *social species*. We are impelled to live together and work collectively to extract from our environment that which we require to sustain ourselves. Social structure emerges, first and foremost, from the demographic, environmental, and biological forces that shape the ways in which we work and live together. While individuals may often be brutal, it is inconceivable that *collectively* males would choose to brutalize females intentionally to shape social structure to their advantage. While human nature is at least partially egocentric, in technologically simple societies self-interest is best served through cooperation and sharing (see Lenski 1966). Today's "altruism" in such societies is returned tomorrow, when sickness, or a bad day at the hunt, or in the gathering process creates need. Under such circumstances, both the social nature of our species and enlightened self-interest mitigate against the wholesale use of force to impose domination by one-half of the species over the other half—especially when the other half gathers the majority of the food available to the collectivity. Since our species evolved as hunter/gatherers and has spent the overwhelming majority of its existence in such societies, it is unlikely that female disadvantage arose initially from superior male strength. Indeed, it is unlikely that it arose from any intentions on the part of men, unlike some other forms of structured inequality, such as slavery. Finally, I also believe that social structures do not persist over long periods of time on the basis of force alone. A substantial degree of support, i.e., legitimacy, is required for a system of inequality to persist. Without it, too many resources would be required to maintain enough fear, to kill off or to isolate enough malcontents, to prevent the overthrow of that system.

So, while scarcely denying the reality of physical coercion in social life, and specifically the use of force by males to intimidate and dominate females, this phenomenon is viewed as an indicator, rather than an explanation of female disadvantage. Where females (or children or slaves) are devalued as people, their superordinates vent their frustrations on them, and the very system of inequality permits them to do so with relative impunity. Moreover, once a system of inequality exists, the use or threat of force buttresses the advantages of the superordinate segment of the population. This is a far cry from arguing that force is an important element in understanding the genesis of female disadvantage, however.

A Final Word on Social Change

The main theme of the theory developed in this book has stressed the importance of a few variables that concern the manner in which societies organize their productive activities to explain the extent to which females are disadvantaged. Social definitional and even family structural variables have been viewed primarily as outgrowths of the work organizational variables, which they buttress through feedback mechanisms. In turn, a series of environmental, demographic, and technological variables are postulated as the key factors that influence the work organization variables. From this perspective, change over time in the dependent variable *Degree of Sex Stratification* is chiefly attributable to changes in one or more of the independent variables, as mediated by their impact primarily on the work organizational variables. Likewise, changes in the family structural and social definitional variables are viewed primarily as the results of changes in the independent variables, as mediated by the work organizational ones.

Implicit in this approach is the assumption that, in the long run, a sort of "equilibrium" among these variables *tends* to arise; that certain modes of organizing work activity, certain family structures, and certain social definitional properties *tend* to become congruent with given demographic, technological and/or environmental realities; and that the result will be a system of sex stratification *tending toward* congruency with the definitional and structural components of a society. It must be emphasized, however, that what is being postulated are *long-term tendencies*. In the shorter run, more-or-less drastic imbalances may exist in the system.

While the organization of work variables may intially give rise to family structural, social definitional, and sex stratification subsystems, once in existence these subsystems take on considerable independence. Stated otherwise, a major technological change, for example, may result in substantial changes in work organizational variables which, eventually, will contribute to change in the other subsystems. These new subsystems, in turn, typically serve to buttress the new forms of work organization. Should yet another change in one or more of the independent variables occur, the independence of the subsystems will serve to resist further changes within themselves. Thus, change will always tend to be uneven; "lag" will always tend to occur; "disequilibrium" will often be apparent. Nonetheless, over time (and the amount of time is probably highly variable), this theory predicts a pattern that entails change in all intervening, as well as the dependent, variables, contingent upon changes in those independent variables. In short, despite the relative independence of the subsystems, their ability to resist change, once the process is initiated, is limited.

In a provocative book, Sanday (1981) argues strongly for the independent impact on the degree of female disadvantage of what have been here termed "social definitional variables." She analyzes religious tenets concerning the sexes, especially creation myths, in 186 technologically simple societies. Her findings from the total sample, as well as the case studies she reports in detail, generally support the relationships posited in this book between work, family, and environmental variables, on the one hand, and social definitional ones, on the other. But she emphasizes the persistence of belief systems and their impact on other structural variables, which tends to reverse the explanatory chain posited in this theory. At a minimum, Sanday's work (along with Bourguignon 1980: 321) serves to remind us that belief systems take on considerable independence from the original conditions that gave rise to them, and are often intractable to change as environmental and structural conditions change.

In the immediately preceding discussion, the units of analysis are "systems" and "subsystems." These are abstractions. In more concrete terms, the process is probably akin to a sociocultural equivalent to natural selection in the biological realm (see Langton 1979). Through differential reinforcement in a given environment, some of the myriad new behavior patterns constantly being generated by individuals (analogous to random mutations in the biological realm) are "selected" to become part of the prevailing culture and social structure. The individuals expressing the behavior initially are rewarded by others in their environment or by success in dealing with their environment. Others perceive this reward process and imitate the behavior until, gradually, it becomes an accepted mode of behavior, i.e., part of the general culture and social structure. Similarly, parts of the established sociocultural system gradually disappear as they become less frequently positively reinforced (or more frequently negatively sanctioned), either by other humans or by success in dealing with the environment.

For example, let us assume that a given society is characterized by large families, i.e., high birthrates are the norm. Some families will, for whatever reasons, be relatively small. In a technologically simple agrarian society, the smaller families will be disadvantaged by the shortage of "hands" to work the fields; i.e., they will fail to receive positive reinforcement and/or they will receive negative reinforcement. Few, if any, others will imitate the behavior, which will be largely the result of "accident," and be perceived by all as unfortunate. Let us suppose, however, that an outside force introduces a highly productive, labor-saving agrarian technology to this society. Suddenly, the few families which are, for whatever reason, small are no longer disadvantaged by their lack of "hands." In fact, they are advantaged by having fewer mouths to feed, hence more per-capita wealth. Their behavior is inadvertently reinforced by success greater than that of their neighbors. Over time, it is likely that their neighbors will perceive this reinforcement and imitate it, and smaller families will eventually become the norm.

This is not to say that the process is always, or even generally, smooth, rapid, or free of conflict. In the example just cited, a whole host of sociocultural supports for large families will have to be overcome. Perhaps new roles will have to be developed for women, who no longer have a large number of children whose care can occupy their lives. Another possible result is a redefinition of how much time and attention each individual child requires, thus raising the per-child investment to compensate for a shrinkage in the total number of children who require care. Religious strictures against birth control may have to be overcome, and one can expect that religious leaders will mount opposition to those who choose to restrict their family size. Social definitions of the two gender roles that link the extent of one's masculinity and/or femininity to number of offspring may also have to be overcome, and new definitions developed.

Regardless of the degree of conflict in the process, it is likely that reinforcement and imitation play a major role in explaining the way system and subsystem change occurs. It should also be noted that the same approach can be used to understand continuity in subsystems. In most societies most of the time, people are rewarded for conformity to collective norms. Thus, even structures and processes which appear punitive to an outside observer (e.g., extensive female disadvantage in a variety of contexts) tend to remain stable over time because societal members reward one another for conformity and punish one another for deviance from prescribed behaviors. From this perspective, then, evolutionary change does indeed occur, but the same mechanisms which explain such change are also responsible for producing relatively strong resistance to change.

To the extent that the explanatory direction postulated by this theory is valid, the ramifications for public policy are clear. Efforts to reduce the extent of female disadvantage are best spent on policies that affect first, the work organizational disadvantages, and second (but nonetheless important), the family structural ones. Such efforts at the governmental level are most likely to be fruitful if they address such variables as technological development, fertility control, alternative child-care institutions, and workplace siting, i.e., the independent variables in this theory. A clear ramification of this approach is that, in the absence of fundamental structural change in the two key sets of intervening variables—those pertaining to the organization of work and to the family—no amount of ideological/religious change, no amount of legislation or political rhetoric, no amount of social movement activism or "consciousness-raising" is going to reduce seriously the overall extent of female disadvantage in any society. To the contrary, structural change is likely to produce definitional and legal changes, and possibly social movement activity, which in turn may speed the process of change in the system of sex stratification.

Finally, as noted several times in this book, change in the extent of female disadvantage does not occur in a linear direction through historical time in a society. There is no long-term, secular trend toward the diminution of female disadvantage—or its increase, either. Societal change in the dependent variable can and has been in both directions over time, females becoming relatively more disadvantaged in some times than was previously the case, and less so in other times.

REFERENCES

Aberle, David D. 1973. "Matrilineal descent in cross-cultural perspective." Pp. 655–730 in David M. Schneider and Kathleen Gough, eds., *Matrilineal Kinship*. Berkeley: University of California Press.

Acker, Joan. 1973. "Women and social stratification: A case of intellectual sexism." *American Journal of Sociology* 78 (January): 936–45.

Ager, Lynn Price. 1980. "The economic role of women in Alaskan Eskimo society." Pp. 305–17 in Erika Bourguignon, ed., *A World of Women*. New York: Praeger.

Almquist, Elizabeth. 1977. "Women in the labor force." *Signs* 2 (Summer): 843–53.,

Amundsen, Kristen. 1971. *The Silenced Majority*. Englewood Cliffs, N.J.: Prentice-Hall.

Andreas, Carol. 1971. *Sex and Caste in America*. Englewood Cliffs, N.J.: Prentice-Hall.

Arizpe, Lourdes. 1977. "Women in the informal labor sector: The case of Mexico City." *Signs* 3: 25–37.

Arrow, Kenneth J. 1973. "The theory of discrimination." Pp. 3–33 in Orley Ashenfelter and Albert Rees, eds., *Discrimination in Labor Markets*. Princeton, N.J.: Princeton University Press.

Averitt, Robert. 1968. *The Dual Economy*. New York: W.W. Norton.

Banfield, Edward C. 1958. *The Moral Basis of a Backward Society*. Chicago: Research Center in Economic and Cultural Change.

_____ . 1968. *The Unheavenly City: The Nature and Future of Our Urban Crisis*. Boston: Little, Brown.

Barrett, Nancy Smith. 1976. "Women in industrial society: An international perspective." Pp. 77–111 in Jane Chapman, ed., *Economic Independence for Women*. Beverly Hills, Calif.: Sage Publications.

Barron, R.D., and G.M. Norris. 1976. "Sexual division and the dual labour market." Pp. 47–69 in Diana Leonard Baker and Sheila Allen, eds., *Dependence and Exploitation in Work and Marriage*. London: Longman.

Becker, Gary S. 1971. *The Economics of Discrimination*. 2nd ed. Chicago, Ill.: University of Chicago Press.

_____ . 1975. *Human Capital*. New York: National Bureau of Economic Research.

_____ . 1976. *The Economic Approach to Human Behavior*. Chicago, Ill.: University of Chicago Press.

Bell, David, Janet Saltzman Chafetz, and Lori H. Horn. 1982. "Marital conflict resolution: A study of strategies and outcomes." *Journal of Family Issues* 3 (March): 111–31.

Bem, Sandra L. 1976. "Probing the promise of androgyny." Pp. 47–62 in A. Kaplan and J. Bean (eds.), *Beyond Sex-Role Stereotypes: Readings Toward a Psychology of Androgyny*. Boston: Little, Brown.

_____ . 1977. "Psychological androgyny." In A. Sargent, ed., *Beyond Sex Roles*. St. Paul, Minn.: West.

Berch, Bettina. 1982. *The Endless Day: The Political Economy of Women and Work*. New York: Harcourt Brace Jovanovich.

Bergmann, B.R., and I. Adelman. 1973. "The 1973 report of the president's Council of Economic Advisors: The economic role of women." *American Economic Review* 63 (September): 509–14.

Bird, Phyllis. 1973. "Images of women in the Old Testament," in R. Ruether, ed., *Religion and Sexism*. New York: Simon & Schuster.

Blau, Peter M. 1964. *Exchange and Power in Social Life*. New York: John Wiley & Sons.

Blood, R., and D. Wolfe. 1960. *Husbands and Wives*. New York: Macmillan.

Blumberg, Rae Lesser. 1978. *Stratification: Socioeconomic and Sexual Inequality*. Dubuque, Iowa: Wm. C. Brown.

———. 1979. "A paradigm for predicting the position of women: Policy implications and problems." Pp. 113–42 in Jean Lipman-Blumen and Jessie Bernard, eds., *Sex Roles and Social Policy*. Beverly Hills, Calif.: Sage Publications.

Bonacich, Edna. 1972. "A Theory of ethnic antagonism: The split labor market." *American Sociological Review* 37 (October): 547–59.

Boserup, Ester. 1970. *Women's Role in Economic Development*. New York: St. Martin's Press; London: Allen and Unwin.

Boulding, Elise. 1976. "The historical roots of occupational segregation." *Signs* 1: 94–117.

Bourguignon, Erika. 1980a. "Introduction and theoretical considerations." Pp. 1–15 in Erika Bourguignon, ed., *A World of Women*. New York: Praeger.

———. 1980b. "Comparisons and implications: What have we learned?" Pp. 321–42 in E. Bourguignon, ed., *A World of Women*. New York: Praeger.

Brown, Judith K. 1970. "Economic organization and the position of women among the Iroquois." *Ethnohistory* 17: 151–67.

Brownmiller, Susan. 1975. *Against Our Will: Men, Women and Rape*. New York: Bantam Books.

Bullough, Bonnie. 1974. "Some questions about the past and the future." Chapter 13 in Vern Bullough, ed., *The Subordinate Sex: A History of Attitudes About Women*. New York: Penguin Books.

Chafe, William H. 1972. *The American Woman*. New York: Oxford University Press.

Chafetz, Janet Saltzman. 1972. "Women in social work." *Social Work* 17 (September): 12–18.

———. 1978. *Masculine/Feminine or Human?* Itasca, Ill.: F.E. Peacock.

———. 1980a. "Conflict resolution in marriage: Toward a theory of spousal strategies and marital dissolution rates." *Journal of Family Issues* 1 (September): 397–421.

———. 1980b. "Theory development, nominal categories and sex roles." *Free Inquiry in Creative Sociology* 8: 21–26.

———. 1980c. "Toward a macro-level theory of sexual stratification and gender differentiation." Pp. 103–25 in S. McNall and G. Howe, eds., *Current Perspectives in Social Theory I*. Greenwich, Conn.: JAI Pub.

Cherry, F., and Kay Deaux. 1975. "Fear of success versus fear of gender-inconsistent behavior: A sex similarity." Paper presented at the Midwestern Psychological Association Meetings, Chicago.

Chincilla, Norma. 1977. "Industrialization, monopoly capitalism, and women's work in Guatemala." *Signs* 3: 38–56.

Chodorow, Nancy. 1978. *The Reproduction of Mothering: Psychoanalysis and the Sociology of Gender*. Berkeley: University of California Press.

Collins, Randall. 1972. "A conflict theory of sexual stratification." In Hans Peter Dreitzel, ed., *Family, Marriage, and the Struggle of the Sexes*. New York: Macmillan.

———. 1973. *Conflict Sociology*. New York: Academic Press.

Coser, Lewis. 1956. *The Functions of Social Conflict*. Glencoe, Ill.: The Free Press.

Cramer, James C. 1980. "Fertility and female employment: Problems of causal direction." *American Sociological Review* 45 (April): 167–90.

Deacon, Desley. 1982. "Women, bureaucracy and the dual labour market: An historical analysis." In Alexander Kouzmin, ed., *Public Sector Administration: Towards Relevance*. Chesire, Melbourne: Longman.

Deaver, Sherri. 1980. "The contemporary Saudi woman." Pp. 19–42 in Erika Bourguingnon, ed., *A World of Women*. New York: Praeger.

Denich, Bette S. 1974. "Sex and power in the Balkans." Pp. 243–62 in M.Z. Rosaldo and Louise Lamphere, eds., *Women, Culture and Society*. Stanford, Calif.: Stanford University Press.

Divale, William T. 1970. "An explanation for primitive warfare: Population control and the significance of primitive sex ratios." *New Scholar* 2: 173–91.

Doeringer, Peter B., and Michael J. Piore. 1971. *Internal Labor Markets and Manpower Analysis*. Lexington, Mass.: D.C. Heath.

Draper, Patricia, and Elizabeth Cashdan. 1975. "!Kung women: Contrasts in sexual egalitarianism in foraging and sedantary contexts." Pp. 77–109 in Rayna Reiter, ed., *Toward an Anthropology of Women*. New York: Monthly Review Press.

Dworkin, Anthony Gary. 1970. "Social Distance and Intergroup Perceptions: Exploratory Research into the Correlates of Stereotypy." Unpublished Ph.D. dissertation, Northwestern University.

Dworkin, Rosalind J. 1976. "A woman's report: Numbers do not a majority make." Pp. 373–99 in A.G. Dworkin and R. Dworkin, eds., *The Minority Report*. New York: Praeger.

Easton, Barbara. 1976. "Industrialization and femininity: A case study of nineteenth century New England." *Social Problems* 23 (April): 389–401.

Elliott, Carolyn M. 1977. "Theories of development: An assessment." *Signs* 3: 1–8.

Ellovich, Risa. 1980. "Dioula women in town: A view of intra-ethnic variation (Ivory Coast)." Pp. 87–103 in Erika Bourguignon, ed., *A World of Women*. New York, Praeger.

Engels, Frederick. 1968. "The origin of the family, private property and the state." Pp. 455–593 in Karl Marx and F. Engels, *Selected Work*. New York: International Pub. (originally published 1884).

Etienne, Mona, and Eleanor Leacock. 1980. "Introduction." Pp. 1–24 in M. Etienne and E. Leacock, eds., *Women and Colonization: Anthropological Perspectives*. New York: Praeger.

Featherman, D.L., and R. M. Hauser. 1976. "Sexual inequalities and socioeconomic achievement in the U.S. 1962–1973." *American Sociological Review* 41 (June): 462–83.

Ferber, M.A., and H.M. Lowry. 1976. "The sex differential in earnings: A reappraisal." *Industrial and Labor Relations Review* 29 (April): 377–87.

Freedman, Marcia, with Gretchen Maclachlan. 1976. *Labor Markets*. Montclair, N.J.: Allanheld, Osmun & Co.

Friedl, Ernestine. 1975. *Women and Men: An Anthropologist's View*. New York: Hold, Rinehart and Winston.

Garske, J. 1975. "Role variation as a determinant of attributed masculinity and femininity." *The Journal of Psychology* 91: 31–37.

Glenn, Evelyn Nakano, and Roslyn L. Feldberg. 1982. "Degraded and deskilled: The proletarianization of clerical work." Pp. 202–17 in R. Kahn-Hut, A. Kaplan Daniels, and Richard Colvard, eds., *Women and Work*. New York: Oxford University Press.

Goldberg, Steven. 1973. *The Inevitability of Patriarchy*. New York: William Morrow.

Gordon, David M. 1972. *Theories of Poverty and Unemployment*. Lexington, Mass.: Lexington Books.

————. 1979. *The Working Poor*. Washington, D.C.: The Council of State Planning Agencies.

Gouldner, Alvin W., and Richard A. Peterson. 1962. *Notes on Technology and the Moral Order*. New York: Bobbs-Merrill.

Guttentag, Marcia, and Paul Secord. 1983. *Too Many Women: Demography, Sex, and Family*. Beverly Hills, Calif.: Sage Publications.

Hacker, Helen M. 1951. "Women as a minority group." *Social Forces* 30: 60–69.

Hacker, Sally. 1982. "Sex stratification, technology, and organization change: A longitudinal case study of AT&T." Pp. 248–66 in R. Kahn-Hat, A Kaplan Daniels, and R. Colvard, eds., *Women and Work: Problems and Perspectives*. New York: Oxford University Press.

Harris, Marvin. 1974. *Cows, Pigs, Wars, and Witches*. New York: Vintage Press.

————. 1975. *Culture, People, and Nature*. 2nd ed. New York: Thomas Y. Crowell.

————. 1977. *Cannibals and Kings*. New York: Random House.

128

Harrison, Bennett, and Andrew Sum. 1979. "The theory of 'dual' or segmented labor markets." *Journal of Economic Issues* 13 (September): 687–706.

Henley, Nancy. 1977. *Body Politics: Power, Sex and Nonverbal Communication.* Englewood Cliffs, N.J.: Prentice-Hall.

Horner, Matina. 1968. "Sex Differences in Achievement Motivation and Performance in Competitive and Non-Competitive Situations." Unpublished doctoral dissertation, University of Michigan.

Howell, Nancy. 1976. "The population of the Dobe Area !Kung." In R.B. Lee and I. DeVore, eds., *Kalahari Hunter-Gatherers.* Cambridge, Mass.: Harvard University Press.

Huber, Joan. 1976. "Toward a sociotechnological theory of the Women's Movement." *Social Problems* 23 (April): 371–88.

Jusenius, Carol. 1976. "Economics" (review essay). *Signs* 2: 177–89.

Kahne, Hilda. 1976. "Women's role in the economy: Economic investigation and research needs." Pp. 39–76 in Jane Chapman, ed., *Economic Independence for Women.* Beverly Hills, Calif.: Sage Publications.

Kanowitz, Leo. 1969. *Women and the Law: The Unfinished Revolution.* Albuquerque, N.M.: University of New Mexico Press.

Kanter, Rosabeth Moss. 1976. "The impact of hierarchial structures on the work behavior of women and men." *Social Problems* 23: 415–30.

————. 1977. *Men and Women of the Corporation.* New York: Basic Books.

Klein, Laura F. 1980. "Contending with colonization: Tlingit men and women in change." Pp. 88–108 in M. Etienne and E. Leacock, eds., *Women and Colonization.* New York: Praeger.

Kohn, Melvin. 1969. *Class and Conformity: A Study in Values.* Homewood, Ill.: Irwin-Dorsey.

Kriesberg, Louis. 1982. *Social Conflicts.* 2nd ed. Englewood Cliffs, N.J.: Prentice-Hall.

Kung, Lydia. 1976. "Factory work and women in Taiwan: Changes in self-image and status." *Signs* 2: 35–58.

Ladner, Joyce. 1972. *Tomorrow's Tomorrow: The Black Woman.* Garden City, N.Y.: Doubleday.

Langton, John. 1979. "Darwinism and the behavioral theory of sociocultural evolution: An analysis." *American Journal of Sociology* 85 (September): 288–309.

Lapidus, Gail Warshafsky. 1976. "Occupational segregation and public policy: A comparative analysis of American and Soviet patterns." *Signs* 2: 119–36.

Laws, Judith Long. 1975. "The psychology of tokenism: An analysis." *Sex Roles* 1: 51–67.

Leacock, Eleanor Burke. 1978. "Introduction." Pp. ix–xxiv in Heleieth Saffioti, *Women in Class Society.* New York: Monthly Review Press.

Leibowitz, Lila. 1978. *Females, Males, Families: A Biosocial Approach.* North Scituate, Mass.: Duxbury Press.

Lenski, Gerhard. 1966. *Power and Privilege: A Theory of Social Stratification.* New York: McGraw-Hill.

————. 1970. *Human Societies.* New York: McGraw-Hill.

Lewis, Oscar. 1965. *La Vida: A Puerto Rican Family in the Culture of Poverty—San Juan and New York.* New York: Random House.

Lorber, Judith, Rose Laub Coser, Alice S. Rossi, and Nancy Chodorow. 1981. "On *The Reproduction of Mothering:* A methodological debate." *Signs* 6 (Spring): 482–514.

Maccoby, Eleanor, and Carol Jacklin. 1974. *The Psychology of Sex Differences.* Stanford, Calif.: Stanford University Press.

Martin, M. Kay, and Barbara Voorhies. 1975. *Female of the Species.* New York: Columbia University Press.

Mayhew, Bruce H. 1980. "Structuralism versus individualism: Part I, Shadowboxing in the dark." *Social Forces* 59 (December): 335–75.

Mead, Margaret. 1935. *Sex and Temperament in Three Primitive Societies.* New York: Dell.

Meeker, B.D., and P. A. Weitzel-O'Neill. 1977. "Sex roles and interpersonal behavior in task-oriented groups." *American Sociological Review* 42: 91–105.

Miller, Casey, and Kate Swift. 1977. *Words and Women: New Language in New Times.* New York: Anchor Books.

Mintz, Sidney. 1971. "Men, women, and trade." *Comparative Studies in Society and History* 13: 266.

Moynihan, Daniel P. 1965. *The Negro Family: The Case for National Action.* Washington, D.C.: U. S. Department of Labor.

Murray, G. F., and M. D. Alvarez. 1975. "Haitian bean circuits: Cropping and trading maneuvers among a cash-oriented peasantry." In S.W. Mintz, ed., *Working Papers in Haitian Culture and Society.* New Haven, Conn.: University Antilles Research Program.

Myrdal, Gunnar. 1944. *An American Dilemma.* New York: Harper & Row.

Nielsen, Joyce. 1978. *Sex in Society: Perspectives on Stratification.* Belmont, Calif.: Wadsworth.

Niethammer, Carolyn. 1981. "Report on the conference on women's contribution to food production and rural development in Africa." *The Women and Food Information Network Newsletter* 3 (December).

O'Kelly, Charlotte G. 1980. *Women and Men in Society.* New York: D Van Nostrand.

Oppenheimer, Valerie K. 1970. *The Female Labor Force in the United States.* Berkeley and Los Angeles: University of California Press.

Pagels, Elaine. 1976. "What became of god the mother? Conflicting images of god in early Christianity." *Signs* 2: 293–315.

Papanek, Hanna. 1977. "Development planning for women." *Signs* 3: 14–21.

Piore, Michael J. 1975. "Notes for a theory of labor market stratification." Pp. 125–50 in R.C. Edwards, M. Reich, and D.M. Gordon, eds., *Labor Market Segmentation.* Lexington, Mass.: D.C. Heath.

Reed, Evelyn. 1975. *Woman's Evolution: From Matriarchal Clan to Patriarchal Family.* New York: Pathfinder Press.

Rosaldo, Michelle Zimbalist. 1974. "Women, culture and society: A theoretical overview." Pp. 17–42 in M. Rosaldo and Louise Lamphere, eds., *Women, Culture and Society.* Stanford, Calif.: Stanford University Press.

Ruether, Rosemary. 1973. *Religion and Sexism: Images of Woman in the Jewish and Christian Traditions.* New York: Simon & Schuster.

Rupp, Leila J. 1977. "Mother of the Volk: The image of women in Nazi ideology." *Signs* 3: 362–79.

Saffioti, Heleieth I.B. 1978. *Women in Class Society.* New York: Monthly Review Press.

Safilios-Rothschild, Constantina. 1970. "The study of family power structure: A review 1960–1969." *Journal of Marriage and the Family* 32: 539–51.

Sahlins, Marshall. 1972. *Stone Age Economics.* Chicago, Ill.: Aldine-Atherton.

Sanday, Peggy R. 1974. "Female status in the public domain." Pp. 189–206 in M. Rosaldo and L. Lamphere, eds., *Women, Culture and Society.* Stanford, Calif.: Stanford University Press.

————. 1981. *Female Power and Male Dominance.* Cambridge: Cambridge University Press.

Scanzoni, L., and J. Scanzoni. 1976. *Men, Women and Change: A Sociology of Marriage and Family.* New York: McGraw-Hill.

Schaffer, Kay. 1981. *Sex Roles and Human Behavior.* Cambridge, Mass.: Winthrop.

Schlegel, Alice. 1972. *Male Dominance and Female Autonomy.* New Haven, Conn.: Human Relations Area File.

Schwartz, Janet. 1980. "Women under socialism: Role definitions of Soviet women." *Social Forces* 58 (September): 67–68.

Scott, Hilda. 1979. "Women in Eastern Europe." Pp. 177–97 in Jean Lipman-Blumen and Jessie Bernard, eds., *Sex Roles and Social Policy.* Beverly Hills, Calif.: Sage Publications.

Semyonov, Moshe. 1980. "The social context of women's labor force participation: A comparative analysis." *American Journal of Sociology* 86 (November): 534–50.

Spence, Janet, and R. Helmrich. 1978. *Masculinity and Femininity.* Austin: University of Texas Press.

Stewart, Abigail J., M. Brinton Lykes, and Marianne LaFrance. 1982. "Educated women's career patterns: Separating social and developmental changes." *Journal of Social Issues* 38: 97–117.

Stoler, Ann. 1977. "Class structure and female autonomy in rural Java." *Signs* 3: 74–89.

Stolzenberg, Ross M., and Linda J. Waite. 1977. "Age, fertility expectations and plans for employment." *American Sociological Review* 42 (October): 769–83.

Stone, Katherine. 1975. "The origins of job structures in the steel industry." Pp. 27–84 in R.C. Edwards, M. Reich, and D.M. Gordon, eds., *Labor Market Segmentation*. Lexington, Mass.: D.C. Heath.

Tickamyer, Ann. 1981. "Wealth and power: A comparison of men and women in the property elite." *Social Forces* 60 (December): 463–81.

Tilly, Louise A., and Joan W. Scott. 1978. *Women, Work, and Family*. New York: Holt, Rinehart & Winston.

Toffler, Alvin. 1980. *The Third Wave*. New York: Bantam Books.

Trey, J.E. 1972. "Women in the war economy—World War II." *The Review of Radical Economics* (July): 1–17.

Unger, Roda K. 1977. "The rediscovery of gender." Paper presented at the Eastern Psychological Association Meetings, Boston.

U.S. Bureau of the Census. 1976. *Statistical Abstracts of the United States*. Washington, D.C.: U.S. Government Printing Office.

Van den Berghe, Pierre. 1973. *Age and Sex in Human Societies: A Biosocial Perspective*. Belmonte, Calif.: Wadsworth.

Vazquez de Miranda, Glaura. 1977. "Women's labor force participation in a developing society: The case of Brazil." *Signs* 3: 261–74.

Veblen, Thorstein. 1953. *The Theory of the Leisure Class*. New York: Mentor Books. (Originally published in 1889.)

Weiner, Annette B. 1980. "Stability in banana leaves: Colonization and women in Kiriwina, Trobriand Islands." Pp. 270–93 in M. Etienne and E. Leacock, eds., *Women and Colonization*. New York: Praeger.

Welch, Finis. 1975. "Human capital theory." *American Economic Review* 65 (May): 63–73.

White, Douglas R., Michael L. Burton, and Lilyan A. Brudner. 1977. "Entailment theory and method: A cross-cultural analysis of the sexual division of labor." *Behavior Science Research* 12: 1–24.

Whyte, Martin King. 1978a. "Cross-cultural codes dealing with the relative status of women." *Ethnology* 17: 211–37.

————. 1978b. *The Status of Women in Preindustrial Societies*. Princeton, N.J.: Princeton University Press.

Yorburg, Betty. 1974. *Sexual Identity: Sex Roles and Social Change*. New York: John Wiley.

Youssef, Nadia H., and Shirley Foster Hartley. 1979. "Demographic indicators of the status of women in various societies." Pp. 83–112 in Jean Lipman-Blumen and Jessie Bernard, eds., *Sex Roles and Social Policy*. Beverly Hills, Calif.: Sage Publications.

INDEX

Aberle, D.D., 57
Access to societal resources, 2, 4–7,
    47–48
Acker, J., 1
Adelman, I., 14
Ager, L.P., 83
Agrarian societies, 36, 52, 57
Almquist, E., 14
Altruism, principle of, 42–43
Alvarez, M.D., 59, 71
Amundsen, K., 50
Andreas, C., 1, 36
Arizpe, L., 64, 65
Arrow, K.J., 74
Attention span, 14, 68–69
Authority, 60, 89–90
Averitt, R., 75

Banfield, E.C., 30
Barrett, N.S., 59
Barron, R.D., 75–76
Becker, G.S., 74
Belief systems, 121
Bell, D., 90
Bem, S.L., 27
Bem Sex Role Inventory (BSRI), 26–27
Berch, B., 14, 53, 54, 55, 59, 62, 65, 69,
    74
Bergmann, B.R., 14
Bilateral, neolocal families, 57
Bird, P., 36
Birth control, 70–71, 97–98
Birthrate, 98–99
Blau, P.M., 31
Blood, R., 90
Blumberg, R.L., 3, 6–8, 13–16, 18, 22, 36,
    42, 53–55, 57, 69, 70, 72, 80, 81, 87,
    89, 98, 100, 101, 119
Bonacich, E., 75
Boserup, E., 64, 95
Bottle-feeding, 98
Boulding, E., 17, 42, 43, 56, 64

Bourguignon, E., 50, 121
Bride price, 80–81
Brown, J.K., 51
Brownmiller, S., 41, 118
Brudner, L.A., 70
Bullough, B., 118
Burton, M.L., 70

Cashdan, E., 64
Chafe, W.H., 63, 72
Chafetz, J.S., 1, 4, 10, 12, 14, 24, 26, 29,
    33, 90
Change, social, 120–23
Cherry, F., 26
Childbearing/child nurturance, 17, 67–72,
    96–99, 110
Chincilla, N., 65
Chodorow, N., 91–92
Class, social, 8–10
Coercion, physical, role of, 118–20
Cohesiveness, male, 19–20
Collectivization of domestic tasks, 69
Collins, R., 118
Colonization, 63–64
Constants, 22, 117–20
Coser, L., 84
Coser, R.L., 91–92
Cramer, J.C., 71
Culture of poverty, 30

Deacon, D., 18, 29, 39
Deaux, K., 26
Deaver, S., 109
Denich, B.S., 84
Disequilibrium, 121
Divale, W.T., 39
Doeringer, P.B., 75
Dowry, 80–81
Draper, P., 64
Dworkin, A.G., 25
Dworkin, R.J., 1

Lewis, O., 30
Lineality, 15, 111
    relative wealth and, 87–88
    restrictions on female behavior and,
        86–87
    work organization and, 55–58. *See also*
        Family structure
Locality, 15, 55–58, 88–89, 111. *See also*
    Family structure
Lorber, J., 91–92
Low-fertility societies, 69–70
Lowry, H.M., 14
Lykes, M.B., 71

Maccoby, E., 27
Maclachlan, G., 75
Marriage, wealth transfer upon, 80–82
Martin, M.K., 3, 15, 18–20, 33, 36,
    42–44, 51, 52, 55–57, 64, 66, 67, 81,
    84–87, 95, 99, 100, 115, 118
Matrilineality, 15, 44–45, 55–56. *See also*
    Family structure
Matrilocality, 15, 55–56
Mayhew, B.H., 4, 21
Mead, M., 10–11, 27
Measures
    of degree of sex inequality, 5–7
    of relative status, 8–10
Meeker, B.D., 30
Miller, C., 36
Mintz, S., 95
Mobility, physical. *See* Physical strength/
    mobility for production
Monogamy, 81–82
Moynihan, D.P., 30
Multivariate analysis, need for, 109
Murray, G.F., 59, 71
Myrdal, G., 1
Myths, origin, 37, 59

Natural selection, 121–22
Nazi Germany, 41
Neocolonialism, 64–65
Nielsen, J., 3, 11, 14, 15, 19, 27, 36, 42,
    43, 58, 115
Niethammer, C., 65
Norris, G.M., 75–76

Occupational segregation, 53–55
O'Kelly, C.G., 3, 16, 36, 37, 52–53, 66,
    69, 80, 81, 83, 95, 98, 99, 103, 115
Oppenheimer, V.K., 62
Origin myths, 37, 59

Pagels, E., 36
Papanek, H., 65
Pastoral societies, 52, 57, 67

Patrilineality, 15, 19–20, 44–45. *See also*
    Family structure
Patrilocality, 15, 19–20
Peterson, R.A., 44, 55, 57–58, 87, 106
Physical strength/mobility for production,
    16–17, 22, 66–67, 93–96, 110
Piore, M.J., 75
Polyandry and polygyny, 81–82
Population density, 20–21, 98–99
    environmental threat/harshness and,
        103–4
    sex ratio and, 72–74, 104–5
    work organization and, 72–74
Postindustrial societies, 62–63
Power, 6, 30, 118–19
Production
    female contribution to, 111–12
    means and products of, ownership/
        control of, 14–15, 46–50, 61–63, 112
    physical strength/mobility for, 16–17,
        22, 66–67, 93–96, 110
    sustenance, 13, 18, 110. *See also* Surplus
        production
Productive/public sphere roles, 13–14,
    58–60
Productive-reproductive activity
    distinction, 16
Property, private, origin of sex inequality
    and, 61–62
Propositional inventory, 109, 110–12
Protective laws, 53

Reed, E., 90
Reinforcement, 121–22
Replaceability, of women's labor, 53–55,
    112
Reproduction of Mothering, The
    (Chodorow), 91–92
Resources, access to, 2, 4–7, 47–48
Roles
    fighting, 40–42
    gender, 10, 24–25
    productive/public sphere, 13–14, 58–60
    reproductive/private sphere, 58–60
    social, 10
    specialization, 26–29
Rosaldo, M.Z., 3, 16
Rossi, A.S., 91–92
Ruether, R., 36
Rupp, L.J., 41

Saffiotti, H.I.B., 65
Safilios-Rothschild, C., 90
Sahlins, M., 18, 60, 101–2
Sanday, P.R., 3, 6, 12, 28, 36–37, 40–43,
    51, 56, 59, 64, 83, 84, 87, 104, 118,
    121
Scanzoni, J., 90

134